The New Bullwhip Book

by Andrew Conway

D1518808

Loompanics Unlimited
Port Townsend, Washington

The New Bullwhip Book

Published by
Loompanics Unlimited
PO Box 1197
Port Townsend, WA 98368
www.loompanics.com
360-385-2230
Fax 360-385-7785

Cover by Jim Blanchard
Interior illos by Andrew Conway

ISBN 1-55950-244-4
Library of Congress Card Catalog Number 2005923720

Contents

For Paula

Chapter One
Introduction

How It Began

For me a bullwhip is the ultimate toy.

The first time I held one, I felt like I was holding a living thing, and a feisty one at that. The slightest motion of the handle made the far end of the whip thrash wildly. A bullwhip is a motion amplifier — move the handle and the tip mirrors that motion a hundred times faster. Change the direction of the handle in just the right way, and you can send a loop rolling down the whip at an ever increasing rate, until the tiny tassel at the far end slices through the air faster than the speed of sound. The crack of the bullwhip is a miniature sonic boom. What other toy goes at Mach 2?

I set out to learn all I could about this fascinating object. I watched other whip crackers, I talked to whip makers, and above all, I practiced. A good way to learn more is to teach others what you have learned, so I started running classes at festivals, and at the San Francisco School of Circus Arts. I compiled an "FAQ," a list of answers to Frequently Asked Questions (which I had been asking not long before) and made this available on the Internet. I made my own whips (they were not very good!) and I even had a master whip maker working in my basement for a while. This book is partly a self-interested attempt to learn some more. However, I hope you can learn a little from it as well.

However much I learn, I will always be a beginner, as there is always something new to learn. Mastering one crack leads to a whole range of variations, which are just as interesting and challenging. Learning a crack with one hand only tempts me to learn it with the other, then with both at once. So, to my fellow beginners, welcome. Let me share with you what I have learned so far, and I hope you will enjoy the journey as much as I have.

The Journey Continues

Well, that was how I introduced the first edition of **The Bullwhip Book** a few years ago. Since then I have been lucky enough to teach some more wonderful students. As always, I've learned from my students as much as they have learned from me. I've also had a chance to spend more time with some of the masters of the art, including visits to my home from Robert Dante and Mike Murphy, and to learn from whip crackers and makers all over the world on the Whip Enthusiasts group on Yahoo.

What all this means is that I now have more to tell you, and I'm lucky that a publisher has stepped up to give me a chance to do so. This is also a chance to correct some of the embarrassing errors in the first edition, which were all too obvious, at least to me!

I'd like to thank all my students at the San Francisco Circus Center and Christian Wysiwyg Filmworks, everyone who read the first edition (especially the people who gave me feedback to improve it), the whip makers who have provided such wonderful toys, the whip crackers who have helped me learn, the San Francisco Academy of Sciences and KPIX Evening Magazine for giving me a chance to show off, and to all the vendors who sold my book. The Whip Enthusiasts Group web address (http://groups.yahoo.com/group/WhipEnthusiasts/) has provided lots of help and information, and a great sense of community. This is a non-political, non-profit educational group that exists for the promotion of sport whip cracking and to provide opportunities to develop whip handling skills. Thanks to the Greenery Press and Loompanics Unlimited who not only publish my ramblings but pay me as well, and to my family for putting up with me. Special thanks to Robert Dante, the only person to give the first edition a bad review, as he inspired me to try harder with this one. You were right, Robert, it was too short. Any remaining errors in the second edition are entirely my responsibility, except for the ones that the publisher puts in just to annoy me.

Chapter Two
Choosing a Whip

This chapter is about the factors you should consider when choosing a single tail whip. If you already own a whip and know the names of all the parts you may wish to skip it, but remember to come back and read it when you want to buy a better one! I believe that even a beginner should buy the best whip that he or she can afford. A bad whip will teach you bad habits, which you will have to unlearn later. You will need to use too much force to crack it, and will get frustrated trying to learn the more technical cracks.

Parts of a Bullwhip

Let me take you on a tour of a whip, starting at the fat end, and working our way towards the skinny bit.

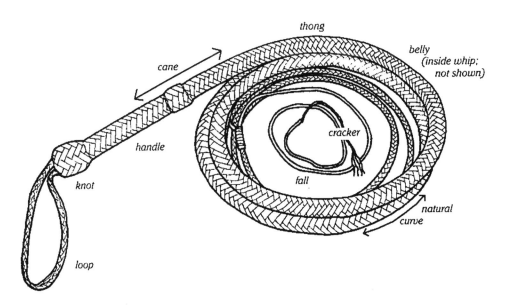

- *The loop.* Attached to the handle there may be a loop. You can put it around your wrist if you like, but some old timers tell us that it is really for hanging the whip for storage. No cowboy would want to risk being pulled from the saddle by his wrist if his whip wrapped round a branch or a fence. I find they get in the way, so I usually cut them off.
- *The knob or knot.* This is the ball on the end of the handle. Braiders call this a knot, and so will I.

- *The handle.* It's pretty obvious which part this is. However, for most cracks you'll be holding the knot, and not the handle.
- *The thong.* This is the braided part of the whip, extending from the handle to the fall. When we talk about the length of a bullwhip, we only consider the length of the thong and the handle. For a stock whip, the handle is ignored, too, and the length is just how long the braided thong is. The idea is that the expensive part is the braiding, so you only have to pay for the part that is braided, and not the fall or popper which are easy to make.
- *The cane.* In a bullwhip the handle and the first part of the thong are stiffened with a rod of cane, fiberglass, or in the old days, whalebone. Whatever the material, this is usually referred to as the cane.
- *The natural curve.* Because of unevenness in the leather and the braiding, most longer leather whips will develop a natural curve. You should always coil it in that direction. I generally arrange the whip in my hand so that when I am about to crack it, it bends in the direction of the natural curve. Some people prefer to go the other way.
- *The belly.* The thong is braided around a belly, which in high quality whips is itself a smaller whip. Sometimes the belly will contain a tapered bag of lead shot to give extra weight to the whip. This is called "shot loading." It's more useful in shorter whips than longer whips, as you need a rapid change in density to make a short whip crack easily.
- *The fall.* At the end of the thong there is usually a single strand of tapered leather called the fall. It will wear away slowly, and needs to be replaced when it gets too short.
- *The popper or cracker.* Attached to the end of the fall is the popper, a few strands of fiber that actually make the crack. These have to be replaced fairly frequently. Some whips designed for hitting do not have poppers, and may have more than one fall attached. You will have a hard time getting a crack out of one of those!

Types of Whip

Many kinds of whips have been developed for different purposes. The three that are most popular and readily available today are snake whips, bullwhips and stock whips. Cow whips have gained quite a bit in popularity since the first edition of this book as they are economical and sturdy.

Bullwhips have a short rigid handle, which gradually becomes more flexible. (See the section above for an illustration.) Originally developed in America for cattle herding, they were used both for making noise and for striking animals. Bullwhips are now made in Australia as well as the U.S., with a thin fall that is more appropriate for noise making than hitting. They typically range in length from four to twenty feet (1.2m to 6m).

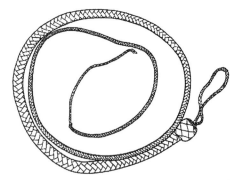

Snake whips are flexible for their entire length. They were designed to be rolled up in a saddlebag. Snake whips as short as three to four feet (0.9m to 1.2m) are very popular, as they can be used in a limited space. However, much longer snake whips can be made. A signal whip is a short snake whip intended to signal to a team of huskies that it is time to get the sled moving. Rules of some sled races prohibit hitting the dogs, so the whips used have to be short enough that they cannot reach the team. Usually the popper is braided directly into the thong without a fall. This makes it hard to replace a popper, so sometimes a popper is made in two parts, one of which can be replaced.

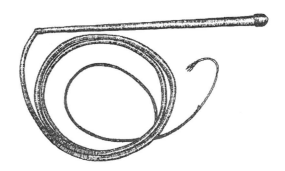

Cow whips originated in Florida. They have a medium length wooden handle typically 14-18 inches (0.35m to 0.45m) in length with the thong entering a socket in the end of it. A couple of strands from the thong appear through a small hole in the side of the handle and are tied round it to hold the whip together. Originally these were made of leather, but the wet conditions in Florida made nylon a better choice, so almost all the cow whips around these days seem to be made of nylon. They handle somewhere between a bullwhip and a stock whip, and come in the same lengths as bullwhips.

Stock whips have a longer handle (called the stock) which is typically 17-21 inches (0.4m to 0.53m) with a little flexibility, connected to the thong by a totally flexible joint. The joint consists of two interlocking leather loops called keepers. These whips normally range from six to ten feet (1.8m to 3m) in length. They were developed in Australia to be used from the saddle as noisemakers and goads while herding stock. It's not entirely clear if the name came from the handle or the cattle. The *Oxford English Dictionary* suggests the latter while some whip makers are adamant that it is the former.

Lunge whips are used for working horses at the end of a long rein. The have a springy handle about six feet (1.8m) long with a thong of similar length, and a thick and heavy popper. The whip does not taper at all. They are machine made and currently sell in tack shops for ten to twenty dollars. Though they are not really intended for technical cracking, you can get them to crack by using that long springy handle to amplify your motions. Many of the cracks in this book will not work with a lunge whip, but I have found the coachman's crack and the Hungarian pig driver's crack work okay.

Whip design is a personal choice. My personal choice is for bullwhips. I like the amount of control I get from the handle, and I enjoy the fact that they involve the whole arm and the whole body, rather than the wristy action of a stock whip. Most of what I'm writing in this book is also applicable to snake and cow whips, though, and to a lesser extent to stock whips.

Materials

The finest whips are made out of kangaroo hide. It is extremely strong, dense, and relatively tolerant of water and abrasion. Cheaper whips are made from cowhide, particularly the tough sorts of leather like latigo, white hide and red hide. These may not last as long or handle as well as a kangaroo hide whip, but they can be an economical way to start cracking. It's worth remembering, though, that a well made and well cared for kangaroo hide whip will last many times as long as a cheap cowhide one, and may be the better bargain in the long run.

Since the first edition of this book, the quality of nylon whips available by mail order or through the Internet has improved dramatically. Several whip makers who work exclusively with nylon parachute cord are making whips that handle almost as well as a good kangaroo hide whip for a third to half the price. There are some drawbacks to nylon. It is lighter than leather, so the belly needs more weight. Leather lace (that's the individual strands of leather) can be cut to taper, but parachute cord cannot. A nylon whip needs to get thinner by dropping strands more frequently than a leather whip. This can give the nylon whip a less even taper, especially in shorter lengths. However, they are an excellent value, and I use them for teaching and recommend them to beginners who may not want to invest in a kangaroo hide whip right away.

Nylon whips tend to be more flexible than leather whips. Whip crackers have differing opinions about this. Some think a nylon whip feels like a really well broken in leather whip, and saves them the trouble of the break in period, while others make slighting comments about wet noodles. If you learn with a nylon whip, I don't think the extra flexibility will be a problem.

Number of Strands and Braiding

Whips can be braided with anything from four to twenty four or more strands. Obviously the more strands you have, the longer the whip takes to make and so the more expensive it is. In return for that, the whip will generally be more lively and responsive. The larger the number of strands, though, the thinner and therefore more fragile each individual strand becomes. A whip with twenty or more strands is likely to be a beautiful collector's item, but unsuitable for heavy everyday use. Whips with eight to sixteen strands seem to be the best compromise between price, durability and responsiveness.

Harder to measure and describe is the quality of the braiding. There should be no kinks or unusual stiffness anywhere in the whip, and it should taper evenly from the handle to the fall. Poorly made whips may taper sharply in the first part of the thong, and then stay almost the same diameter for the rest of their length. The lace should be cut so that all the strands at the same part of the whip are the same width. None of the strands should be wider than others.

The Belly

Perhaps the most important part of a good whip is the part you can't see, the belly. This is partly because it is easy to cut corners on something that is out of sight! A good belly is itself a smaller braided whip, and may even have another whip inside that. A cheap belly will have strips of leather, which do not flex as well, or even rope or paper, which do not provide enough weight change as the whip tapers. A good belly may have a layer of calfskin covering it; a cheaper one may be wrapped in electrical tape.

The best way to make sure that your whip has a well-constructed belly is to follow the old Australian adage, "Never buy a whip from someone you don't trust."

Texas and Australian Falls

Some shorter whips have the popper braided directly onto the end of the thong, but on longer whips there is usually a fall of some sort. You may find a strip of thin leather about three quarters of an inch (2cm) wide and a foot or two (0.3m to 0.6m) long, without any taper. This is a Texas style fall. It is better for hitting livestock with, as the broader surface will not cut flesh the way a narrow fall will. Even if it has a popper on the end, it is not very good for cracking, as the wide fall acts like a brake in the air. You can improve the cracking performance of a Texas fall by using a sharp blade to trim it so it tapers from its full width at the end of the thong down to about a quarter of an inch (6mm) where the popper is attached.

Australian falls are a strand of thicker leather, cut so that they are circular (or at least hexagonal) in cross section, and tapering smoothly from the thong to the popper. The diameter of the start of the fall should be the same as the diameter of the end of the thong, so that the motion of the whip is transferred smoothly from one to the other. The fall itself should taper smoothly to as fine a point as the leather can take without breaking when the whip is cracked, to increase the amplification of the whip's motion. I have had the performance of a whip improve dramatically when I put a better quality fall on it.

The better the quality of leather, the finer the fall can be tapered. A low quality fall will have a square cross section, not much taper, and the end will fly off when you crack the whip too loud. A good fall will have a round cross section, taper to a fine point and take weeks or months of use before the knot at the end comes off. Sometimes a beginning whip maker will have trouble finding strong enough leather to make good falls. The Aussie old timers say that the strongest leather comes from a cow that has died out in the bush, and not been discovered for a few weeks. (The meat, however, is not so good!)

There are a couple of types of nylon falls that you may see. One is a single strand of parachute cord. These do not amplify the motion of the whip, and will act as a break if they are too long. They are fine at a length of six inches (0.15m) or so. The second sort is two strands of parachute cord twisted together. These are better for transferring the motion of the whip to the popper, and some whip makers even manage to taper them by removing some of the parachute cord's core.

Swivel Handles

American cowboys frequently used the overhead crack. This involves swinging the whip round and round in the air above your head. To let this happen without the whip twisting, it was often attached to the handle with a bearing that allowed it to rotate. This swivel handle can still be found on some American bullwhips today. It's usually seen on the cheaper latigo whips, though there are one or two whip makers who would be happy to make a high quality whip with a swivel handle if you want one.

Unless you want to concentrate on overhead cracks to the exclusion of other forms of cracking you do not need a swivel handle. You should certainly avoid it if you want to concentrate on accuracy, as the rotation of the whip on the handle adds another variable to a situation where you are trying to keep everything as nearly the same as possible.

Length

It is tempting for a beginner to start with a very short whip. They are generally cheaper and they take less space to use. However, there are some other factors to consider. Shorter whips are more dangerous to use, as they move faster and crack closer to your face. There is less time to recover from a mistake than there is with a longer whip.

It is also easier to crack a small whip using brute force, rather than the correct style. If you really wish to develop your whip cracking skills, I suggest you start out with a longer whip, about six to eight feet (1.8m to 2.5m) in length. Longer whips than that are hard for a beginner to control, and shorter whips are too fast to be safe, and can teach bad habits.

The illustrations and descriptions in this book assume you are using a bullwhip about six to eight feet (1.8m to 2.5m) long. With a longer whip things will move more slowly, and your motions must be larger. With a short whip, everything moves faster, and your motions must be smaller — a movement of the whole arm becomes a move of the forearm, a movement of the forearm becomes a twist of the wrist.

If you do decide to buy a shorter whip, and have a limited space in which to practice, then you should probably concentrate first on the sidearm crack and its variations, as these work well under a low ceiling.

Workmanship

Even with the same materials and design, there are many tiny factors that can turn a good whip into a great one. In cutting the hide for example, a poor workman may use a mechanical lace cutter, while a master craftsman will cut each strand by hand, avoiding weak spots in the leather, adjusting the width of the strands to compensate for variations in stretchiness and making sure that the parts of the whip that take the most stress are braided from the strongest part of the hide. In braiding, each strand must be pulled with exactly the correct tension, and as the whip tapers, strands must be dropped in a way that does not introduce any sudden change in diameter or stiffness.

All this contributes to the "life" of a whip. To test how lively a whip is, hold the knot up high and let the whip hang vertically downwards. Give the knot a gentle shake, and see how rapidly that motion is transmitted to the popper, and how large the motion is by the time it gets there. The more responsive a whip is, the better.

There are now a number of whip makers with web pages selling their goods directly to the public, alongside the more established distributors like David Morgan and Western Stage Props. It can be hard to know from a web page if you are dealing with a master craftsman or an opportunist selling shoddy work for whatever the market will bear. I have heard from several people who have ordered whips over the Internet from Australia and have waited years without receiving their orders. If you do order internationally, I would strongly advise you to only order from a current member of the Australian Plaiters and Whipmakers Association. While this is no guarantee of quality, they will expel any member who does not follow ethical business practices. Their newsletter *The Australian Whipmaker* publishes the results of the whip making competitions at the Sydney Royal Show and other events. If you buy a whip from the winner (or the judge!) of one of these competitions you can be sure it will be a quality product.

Chapter Three
Whip Cracking Basics

Your New Whip

Now that you have your whip, I'm sure that you'd like to get cracking right away. However, there are a few basic concepts that I'd like to go over first, so that you will know what I am talking about.

If you have purchased a leather whip, it may have dried out in storage, or on its way to you. It's a good idea to put some conditioner on it before you use it. See Chapter Thirteen on caring for your whip.

A new leather whip will be a little stiff at first, and some people like to break them in by oiling, flexing or rolling them. I recommend against this, as it will shorten the life of the whip. The best way to break a whip in is to use it as it was intended. As it gradually becomes more flexible, so your style will change to compensate. Nylon whips generally start out more flexible than leather whips, and won't need any breaking in.

Components of a Crack

I'd like to break each crack down into three stages: the setup, the turn and the follow through.

- *The setup* creates the initial conditions for the crack. In some cases this is just positioning the whip correctly, but in others, you must set up both the position and the motion of the whip so that it is ready to crack.
- *The turn.* Here you change the motion of the whip in some way. The speed of this change is amplified by the taper of the whip, and causes the crack.
- *The follow through* is what you do with the whip after it has cracked. This can be to position it for the next crack, prevent it from recoiling in your face or simply to look graceful.

Making the whip crack does not require a lot of physical strength. Instead, it requires precise and graceful movements. Whip crackers talk about using "form" rather than "muscle," and to say that someone is muscling a whip is to imply that they lack skill. However, low quality whips will require a little more muscle than good whips to get a crack out of them.

You must always guide the whip, using the knot, rather than forcing it using the handle. Let the whip do the work for you. Putting too much bending force on the handle will weaken the whip at the start of the thong. It's especially important for snake whips that you always hold them by the knot, as the entire whip is designed to flex. Grasping a snake whip by the end of the thong rather than the knot places undue stress on the point where the thong leaves your hand.

In this book I will repeatedly talk about the plane of the crack. For a good crisp crack, it is important that all the motion of the whip takes place in a single plane. The plane may be vertical, horizontal or tilted, but the whip should be confined as closely as possible to two dimensions, not three. Now clearly, when there is a loop in the whip it will need a little space in the third dimension, but if what you have is a helix (that is, a corkscrew shape) then you will only get a weak crack, or no crack at all. You can change from one plane to another for consecutive cracks, but only during the follow through of the first crack, before the setup of the second crack.

While there are standard names for the parts of a whip, the names for different cracks are not so well defined — the same crack may have several different names and different cracks may have the same name when you talk to different people. The names in this book are the ones I use, but don't expect anyone else to agree with them, unless they have read the same book! Where there are other common names I will mention them, especially if they are the ones used in Australian whip cracking competitions.

The Space You Crack In

Here are a few simple terms for parts of the space that you are cracking in, so that I can describe the various cracks.

First of all, I would like you to imagine that you are standing facing a wall, a short distance in front of your nose. The plane of this wall we will call the "front wall plane."

Turn 90 degrees to the left or right so that the wall touches your shoulder. This is now your "shoulder wall plane." Obviously, you have one shoulder wall plane on each side of your body. There is also a rear wall plane, though we won't be using that very much in this book.

Now imagine you are standing in a swimming pool with the water up to your waist. The surface of the water I call the "belt plane." If the water were about six inches (15cm) over your head, then its surface would be the "helicopter plane." (Yes, I know a helicopter isn't really a plane, but just think of the blades of a helicopter spinning over your head and you'll get the idea.)

I've tried to avoid the terms "left" and "right" as I think it's a good idea to learn whip cracking with both hands. Instead I will use the terms "whip side" and "other side." Obviously, the hand that is holding the whip is on the whip side of your body.

The Physics of Whips

Good whips are designed so that they taper evenly from the handle to the popper. The shape is not important, but the distribution of mass is. If you change the motion of the handle, that change is transmitted down the length of the whip. The energy you apply to moving the handle ends up moving the popper instead. Some of the energy is dissipated in friction, but much of it ends up accelerating that little tuft of nylon. Now, the less mass an object has, the faster it has to go to have the same amount of kinetic energy, so the popper ends up travelling much faster than the handle.

You can also describe this motion amplification in terms of conservation of angular momentum, or if you want to be really precise, you can write down partial differential equations that define an idealized bullwhip, but the result is the same. When you accelerate the handle, that energy is transmitted to the popper with the motion being amplified many times over.

I'm using the word "acceleration" in the scientific sense of being a change in speed or direction. You're not putting any energy into the whip if you just keep it moving in the same direction at the same speed (apart from the little needed to overcome friction.) In order to get a crack either the speed or direction of motion of the handle must change. In describing cracks, this is what I call the "turn." Sometimes the acceleration can even be a negative change in speed. In the sidearm crack, for example, it is the fact that the handle stops moving that sends a wave of energy down the whip and causes it to crack.

Until this century, nobody really knew why whips cracked. One theory was that the tip of the popper folded back and hit itself. However, high-speed photography has shown us that this is not so. Instead, it has been discovered that the popper ends up travelling at twice the speed of sound. It's now generally agreed that the crack of a whip is a miniature sonic boom, caused by the shock wave that builds up when the leading edge of the loop traveling down the whip breaks the sound barrier. If the loop is traveling at the speed of sound and the bottom of the loop is not moving because you are holding the other end of the whip in your hand, then the top of the loop is going at twice the speed of sound.

If you want to find out more about the physics of whip cracking, the classic article that proved that whips go faster than sound is "On the dynamics of a bullwhip," by Bernstein, Hall and Trent in the *Journal of the Acoustical Society of America*, Vol. 30, No. 12, December 1958. Assisting in the research was a troupe of artists called Los Larabees. There are further references to scientific papers about bullwhips in Wolfgang Schebeczek's Bibliographic Notes in *Kaskade* No. 42, Summer 1996. More recent mathematical research on the motion of whips can be found in the work of A. Goriely and T. McMillen of the University of Arizona, particularly "Whip waves" Physica D, 2003 and "The shape of a cracking whip" Phys. Rev. Lett 2002, 88, # 244301. Dr. Goriely did not have any circus artists to help in this work, but he did learn to crack a whip himself, and also built a machine to make a consistent crack so that he could take high speed films.

Keeping a Safe Space

A bullwhip can cut flesh, break bones or put out an eye. However, it is only that dangerous for a brief interval in space and time, right at the tip of the whip just as it is cracking. Your job is to keep that crack well away from anything valuable, especially yourself. At other times in its flight it can still leave a serious welt, so you should be aware of all its movements.

The Danger Zone

The danger zone for a bullwhip is a hemisphere, with you at the center. It extends all around you and up into the air over your head for the full length of the whip including the fall and popper, plus the length of your arm. For an eight-foot (2.5m) whip you need to monitor a circle about twenty five feet (8m) across, and be on the look out for tree branches or power lines up to twenty feet (6m) in the air. Be especially aware of the space behind you. A person could walk into that space and be caught by your whip on a back swing. I confess that only today I managed to overturn a mic stand which had wandered up behind me while I wasn't looking.

Your danger zone also extends for some distance beyond the length of the whip in the direction you are cracking it. Sometimes the knot at the end of the fall may break off, travelling faster than the speed of sound — so don't crack towards people. Don't practice on surfaces with loose materials on them, as the popper can pick up gravel, twigs or grit and fling them off at high speed.

Don't leave a whip lying on the ground where you or someone else may tread on it or trip over it. When you have finished using a whip, make a habit of coiling it loosely and putting it back in your toy bag.

Protective Gear

You should protect yourself against a wandering whip by wearing appropriate clothing and protective gear. How much you wear should depend on how comfortable you are with the cracks you are working on. If you are completely in control of a particular move, and it is a relatively safe one such as the forward crack, then you may not feel the need to bother with much protection. However, when you are starting to work on any new crack, you should make yourself as safe as possible. Here's what I recommend:

- *Eye protection.* This is a must for any crack that is new to you. Glasses or sunglasses will do, but plastic goggles from the hardware store are better.
- *Head protection.* I've been known to wear a hard hat with ear covers and a mesh faceplate when working on a crack that went right past my face. A motorcycle helmet also provides full head protection. However, most of the time I settle for a hat with a stiff brim that projects all around. This saves me from the risk of a notch in my ear from an errant popper, without being too cumbersome on my head. Cowboy hats work very well for this. Coincidence?
- *Gloves.* The first time you practice for an hour or two, you will probably get blisters on your hands from the whip handle. Any sort of gloves will prevent this, but leather work gloves will also protect you from the other end of the whip. You can also put up with the blisters for a few weeks and you will grow calluses on your palms and not have to worry about abrasion any more.
- *Clothing.* Cute as you look in those tight shorts, bare skin is not a good idea when you are learning to crack a whip. Thick pants and a stout jacket are much more sensible, and leather clothes are the best. I usually settle for a flannel shirt with long sleeves and corduroy pants. Every time I practice in a T-shirt I end up regretting it.
- *Ear plugs.* If you are cracking a whip indoors, you may find it is painfully loud. Even if it is not painful, prolonged exposure to loud noises is not good for your ears, so you may wish to wear earplugs. Me, I'm planning on going deaf in my old age. My kids don't listen to a word I say these days, so in a couple of decades I'm going to return the compliment.
- *Eye protection.* This one is really important, so I thought I'd mention it again. Don't come looking for me if you blind yourself.

I know that the illustrations in this book do not show protective gear, but they are highly paid stunt illustrations who never make mistakes.

Practicing in Public

One of the problems of bullwhip ownership is finding a place to practice. A large indoor space like a gym or hall is best; a racquetball court will do (though the enclosed space and hard walls make it very noisy). If you don't have access to either of these, you may be forced to work out of doors, in your back yard or in the local park.

If you are practicing in a public park, be on the lookout for dogs, as they can run rapidly and unpredictably into your danger zone. Some dogs are frightened by whips, so it is a good idea to stop practicing for a moment if a nervous looking dog walks by.

Always be aware that not everyone enjoys the sound of a whip as much as you do. Don't crack your whip too loudly; this is bad for the whip as well as being annoying for others. Stay as far away from other folks as possible, and if anyone asks you to move somewhere else and you can reasonably do so, then move along.

Sometimes someone will complain to the police about the crazy guy with the whip that is attacking the vegetation and scaring the squirrels. Always be polite to the cops, and take along a copy of this book, so that you can show them where it says that whip cracking is a healthy outdoor sporting activity that builds strong bones and teeth.

Whip cracking is a healthy outdoor sporting activity that builds strong bones and teeth, officer.

Finally, if you are around other people who are cracking whips, don't enter their danger zone unless you have warned them first.

Chapter Four
Three Basic Cracks

If you're like me, you've skipped all the chapters before this one, since you really want to learn how to crack that whip. That's okay, so long as you wear eye protection, and go back and read the chapter on safety the first time you hurt yourself. Also, if you don't understand any of the terms I used, look them up in the earlier chapters.

In this chapter, I'll be telling you about three basic cracks that we will use as the building blocks for more advanced work. You should master all of them.

The Forward Crack

The first crack you should learn is the one I call the forward crack. It has various other names, though. I've heard it called the circus crack and the gypsy crack. In Australia they call something very similar the cattleman's crack.

There are several reasons why this is a good place to start. First of all, it is a relatively safe crack. The whip is not going too fast when it goes past your body, and it goes from back to front. If you do mess up and hit yourself it won't be in the face. After the whip cracks, the follow through takes it down to the ground and not back towards your body. There's nothing that makes you feel a fool faster than a really impressive crack followed by a face full of whip.

The second reason I like to teach this to beginners, is that it is such a useful crack. In fact, I have seen a five-minute stage routine by a whip artist who did nothing but slight variations on the forward crack! You can use it just to make a sound, you can cut targets with it, you can put out candles or you can use it to wrap a horizontal object such as an assistant's arm. The whip travels through a large vertical plane (the shoulder wall plane) and anywhere that a target intersects that plane the whip will cut it. This means that as well as having an assistant hold a target, you can also hold one yourself — behind your back, over your head or even in your mouth.

The third reason is that it is a fundamental building block for more complex moves. When you have mastered the forward crack, you can move on to the reverse crack, figure eights, fast figure eights and volleys.

If your whip has a natural curve (most long leather whips do, many nylon whips do not) then you must now decide if you want to crack with the natural curve or against it. By cracking with the curve, I mean that the final loop that will make the crack, coils the whip in the same direction it curls naturally. If you are cracking against the curve you are flexing the whip in the opposite direction. Some whip handlers are almost religious over this issue, and debates on the topic can get very heated.

If you crack with the natural curve you will exert less energy, and you will generally have a more graceful and fluid style. If you crack against the natural curve, you will be putting more effort into the crack, but the result will be louder and more macho. My suggestion is that you experiment and find out what works best for you, and then stick with that. I have heard it suggested that cracking one way or another will wear a whip out faster, but I believe this is a misconception.

Whichever way you decide to go, the natural curve should always lie in the plane in which the whip is cracking. Never twist the handle of the whip so that the natural curve forces the motion of the whip out of the plane of the crack. This is true for almost all cracks, and not just the forward crack.

In this crack, as in most others, the final push that helps the whip to crack comes from the thumb (or the V between the thumb and index finger if you prefer that grip). If you want to crack with the natural curve you should hold the handle so that your thumb is on the inside of this curve. If you crack against the natural curve your thumb should be on the outside.

I will break this crack down into the usual three phases, the setup, the turn and the follow through.

The Setup

Take the knot in the palm of your hand, with your thumb pointing down the handle. I find it most comfortable to have the knot right in the middle of my palm, but some people prefer it further back towards the wrist, especially if using a stock whip. Don't grasp the middle of the handle, though. Hold your arm straight down, with the handle of the whip pointing downwards and your thumb at the front. Arrange the whip so that it is lying in a line directly behind your whip hand. If you want the final crack to be with the natural curve, the whip should now be flexed against the natural curve, and vice versa.

Getting the whip in a straight line behind you is not easy at first. It always seems to shoot over further than you expect, or try to squirm around like an eel. The simple way to straighten out any curves in the whip is to lay it out behind you anyhow and then take a pace or two forward, but with a little practice you will find that you can flip the handle gently so that the thong moves into the right position. If you start with the handle pointing forward, and then rotate it until it points upward and then backwards, keeping it in the shoulder wall plane, you will send a loop down the whip which will straighten it out. You may wish to spend a few minutes practicing this just to get to know your whip before you try to crack it. If you don't get the whip straight, don't wear shorts! Enough said.

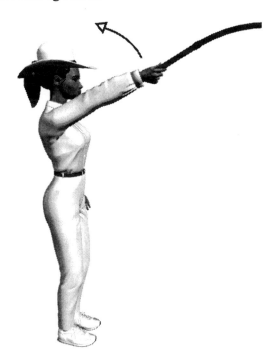

Now, keeping your arm straight, swing it forwards, and upwards, all the time keeping it in the shoulder wall plane. The tip of the whip will make a big circle, **UP** in front of you. You should be going fast enough to keep the whip straight in the air. This is the time when you are putting most of the energy into the whip, which will later be released in the crack. Work, says the physicist, is force times distance. This means you don't have to exert a huge amount of force to get a whip to crack, you just have to apply that force over a large distance. Make sure you are using a big arm motion if you are using a bullwhip or a snake. With a stock whip or a cow whip the handle acts as a lever, so you can use a smaller arm motion, and apply more twisting force with your wrist.

When your arm is horizontal allow your elbow to bend upwards, and let your wrist tilt backward so that the whip can continue its motion **OVER**. Eventually the whip will once again be pointing straight backwards, but this time it will be in the air at about shoulder level. Do not let your elbow swing out to the side; keep it pointing forwards.

The Turn

When the whip is behind you in the air you need to propel it straight forward. By now your elbow should be bent at a right angle so that your upper arm is horizontal, pointing forward in the shoulder wall plane, and your forearm is vertical. Don't bend your elbow much more than ninety degrees, though, or let your hand go too far back.

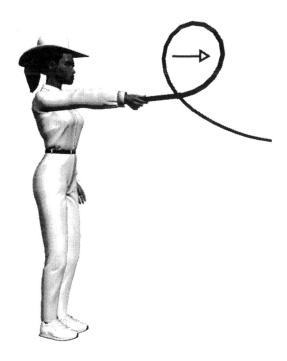

Now, drop your elbow slightly so that your hand is just above shoulder height, and then push your hand straight **FORWARD**. Straighten your elbow until your whole arm is horizontal, and then tilt your wrist so that the handle of the whip points forward. The whip will come past your body, just outside your shoulder and arm. A loop will form, which will roll forward along its length. You do not need to put a tremendous amount of force into this part of the crack, just enough to change the direction of the whip. All the energy that you stored in the whip during the setup is ready to be released, you just need to direct it.

Chapter Four
Three Basic Cracks

The Follow Through

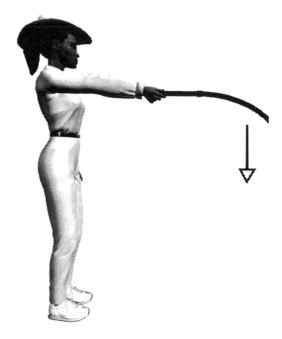

Just keep your arm pointing straight forward without moving until the whip **CRACKS**. The whip should crack in the shoulder wall plane well in front of you and a few feet (0.5m-1m) above your head, then fall to the ground, its force exhausted. Now you can bring your arm back down to pull the whip back **DOWN** and position it behind you for another crack.

What Went Wrong?

The chances are the first few times you try this you will not get very many cracks, or the whip may be cracking in the wrong place. Watch for the loop that rolls along the whip. If it is a small loop in the shoulder wall plane rolling straight forward then your whip will crack. If you don't see this then you're probably having one of the following problems:

- *The whip was not lined up at the start.* If you find that you are hitting yourself on the back of the legs it may be because the whip did not start up in a line behind your whip hand. Get in the habit of checking the alignment of the whip every time you crack, especially if you are using anything longer than a six-footer.
- *Snatching.* You will not see the loop at all, because the whip is cracking next to your ear rather than well in front of you. You are starting the turn too early and pulling the whip down rather than forward. Make sure the setup places the whip all the way behind you before you start the turn, and don't try to apply too much force during the turn.
- *Hesitation.* This is the opposite of snatching. After the setup you stop to think about what you are doing, and allow the whip to lose all its momentum before going into the turn. You'll probably do this a few times when you are learning, but then get over it. It may help you to vocalize as you crack, that is, say to yourself something like "Up, over, back, forwards, crack, down," as you go through the motions. This will help you to get your timing consistent. I once taught a belly dancer to crack a whip, and she assigned a note to each position, and then sang her way thought the crack. She learned very quickly.

- *Leaving the shoulder wall plane.* There are several warning signs for this. If you are hitting yourself on the back, if the loop is not in a vertical plane but pulled out into a helical spring shape, or if the follow through brings the whip back across the front of your body, then you are not keeping the motion of your arm in the shoulder wall plane. You are almost certainly sticking your elbow out to the side! Keep all the motions of your arm in the shoulder arm plane, and the whip will stay there too. There should be no sideways motion of your elbow at all. (You can check this by making your usual cracking motion while facing a mirror. Watch that elbow!)

- *Leaving the shoulder wall plane.* Yes, I know I just warned you about this one, but you're probably still doing it. Almost everyone does when they are learning this crack. Is the follow through still hitting you on the shins? Then you are still letting your elbow creep out to the side at the end of the setup. Stop it!

- *Leaving the shoulder wall plane, one more time.* You've watched yourself in a mirror and your elbow motion is perfect, but the whip is still not cracking properly and is hitting your legs in the follow through. Okay, now it's time to watch the angle at which you are holding the handle. Wherever you are in the motion of the whip, the handle should be tilted just slightly away from your body, and your palm should be facing inwards. Don't twist your hand, and don't tilt the whip towards your body when it is over your head.

- *Going back over the top.* It's important that the turn should propel the whip straight forward. Don't try to take the whip back in a circle, reversing the motion of the setup. The fall and popper should stay pointing downward during the turn. If they flip back upward before the crack, check your arm motion carefully.

- *Finishing too low.* Your arm should be perfectly horizontal and pointing forward after the whip has cracked. If you arm is pointing downward it will be harder to crack the whip, and you risk damaging it by hitting it on the ground. Check your arm position after each crack and make sure it is okay.

- *Missing popper.* The last crack may have been so hard that the cracker has left the whip, possibly taking some of the fall with it. You can get a crack with just the fall, but it is more difficult and will chew up your fall in no time.

- *Knots.* Sometimes your whip may manage to wriggle itself into a knot, especially in the fall or popper. You may get hitches, figure eight knots, blood knots, slip knots and plain old tangles. If you go on cracking with a knot in your whip it will just get tighter and tighter, so untie it right away. It's a good idea to glance at your whip after every crack to make sure there are no knots.

- *Timing.* If everything else is perfect but the loop is too big, then you have a timing problem. Some part of your motion is too fast or too slow. Get a friend to watch you, and tell you where the whip is when you start the turn. With a whip that is six foot or under it should be horizontal in the air behind you. If it slopes upward from your hand, then you are starting the turn too early, and if it slopes downward you are too late. With a whip that is eight foot or more you can afford to wait until you hear the fall touch the ground behind you before you begin the turn.

Are you feeling comfortable with the forward crack? Is the whip cracking effortlessly every time, with a satisfying pop that is not too loud but speaks of great power under precise control? Right, now try it with your other hand. It's a great way to demonstrate how much you have actually learned, and besides, some day you're going to want to work on that really cool two-handed stuff, so you might was well start now.

The Sidearm Crack

This crack, with its variants, is another useful and versatile whip move. You can use it to cut targets or to wrap a volunteer. It works under a low ceiling, too, so you can use it in places where a forward crack would be impractical. It is harder to learn than the forward crack, and a little more dangerous. A bad setup and you will lash the back of your legs, and a careless follow through can bring the whip right back in your face. This crack is well worth the effort to master, though.

There are several forms of the sidearm crack, but the one I will describe first happens with the whip moving in the belt plane.

The Setup

Stand with your whip side foot a little behind your other foot. Take the knot in the palm of your hand, with your arm extended downward, outward, and a little behind your body. Turn your wrist so that your palm is facing upward with your thumb pointing along the inside of the handle. Arrange the whip in a straight line behind you on the ground, with the inside of the natural curve towards your thumb. (If you prefer you can have your forefinger along the handle rather than your thumb.)

Lift the handle by bending your elbow, and push the whip straight forward with the knot first. I like to take a step forward with my whip side foot during this crack.

Chapter Four
Three Basic Cracks

As the whip comes past you, let the handle rotate in the belt plane. Push on the back of the handle with your thumb to give it some extra momentum. This should form a U-shape in the whip, travelling forward in the belt plane.

Leave your arm extended forward until the whip cracks.

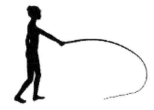

The Follow Through

After the crack, bring your arm across to the other side of your body, so that the whip does not recoil into your face.

Turn your wrist so that your palm is facing downward and allow the whip to fall behind you on the other side of your body. You are now in the starting position for the backhand version of the sidearm crack, which I will be describing later!

Alternative Follow Through

Another way to finish this move is to bring the whip back over your head. As the whip cracks raise your hand, and guide the whip upwards and over to the other side.

Let the thong pass over your head, and the fall and popper travel by the other side of your body. Guide the whip so that it falls in a line behind you on the whip side. You are now in exactly the position in which you started, and ready to do another sidearm crack.

What Went Wrong?

It may take a number of tries before you can get the sidearm crack to work, and even more practice before you can get it to work every time. Generally it is easier with longer whips, and more difficult with shorter ones, unless they are of high quality.

- *Hitting the back of legs*. This can be painful, and even worse, embarrassing! It usually happens because you did not have the whip in a straight line behind you before you started the crack.
- *Dragging*. If you do not lift the whip up as you start to move it forward, it will drag on the floor, which may slow it down enough to prevent it cracking, especially if you are on a rough surface like grass.
- *Leaving the belt plane*. The U-shape you make with the whip should only be tilted slightly out of the horizontal plane. Don't let it slope down too much.
- *Swinging*. Watch the U-shape as it rolls forward. It should be as narrow as possible. If it is wide, that is because you swung your arm in an arc rather than pushing the whip straight forward. If you are doing it right you will have to tuck your elbow in toward your body as the whip handle passes you, to compensate for the fact that the natural motion of your arm is circular rather than a straight line.
- *Knots*. I used to think that if I could learn to be a really good whip cracker, I would never get knots in my whips. Then I heard Alex Green, who did the whip stunts in *The Mask of Zorro*, speaking at a Wild West Arts Club convention. He said that whenever he was doing a live show, he took along two of every whip that he was going to be using, so that if he got a knot in one, he could switch to the other. I felt better about my knots then.

- *Hitting the face*. Ouch! I hope you remembered to wear eye protection. You were probably so excited by getting the whip to crack that you forgot to follow through.

The Overhead Crack

This crack takes up lots of space, but it is one of the showiest, and potentially loudest of all cracks. You may find it a little frightening the first few times you try it. The whip may seem determined to wrap itself around your head. If you're nervous, that will interfere with your ability to crack the whip smoothly, because you will hesitate or go too slowly. This, of course, makes it more likely that you will hit yourself. You can escape from this vicious circle by wearing a motorcycle helmet, so you don't have anything to be afraid of.

You may think of this crack as being the forward crack tilted over ninety degrees so that it is in a horizontal plane, as the arm motion is similar. In fact, you can sneak up on it by doing a forward crack while tilting your body further and further away from the whip side. If you can tilt your body at right angles from your legs, your arm will be making the right motion. Now straighten your body up again while leaving your arm doing the same thing. If that sounds too hard, you can just follow the instructions below.

First of all there are some warm up exercises you should do. Swing the whip around above your head, first in one direction for a few turns, then stop and try the other direction. Make sure that the whip is moving in a horizontal plane, and not sloping from front to back. Use a big arm motion. Remember that bit about work being force times distance? Once again, by using your whole arm and not just your wrist you can put lots of energy in the whip with very little force. Once you are comfortable with twirling the whip in both directions, all you have to do is learn to change directions in just the right way. Here we go.

Using a full arm motion, swing the whip around above your head in the helicopter plane. Imagine you are standing on a big clock face, facing the twelve. If the whip is in your right hand, it should be going counterclockwise, and if it is in your left hand, clockwise. You can go around as many times as you like, but when practicing it is good to be consistent, so I would suggest always making just two revolutions. When the whip is pointing directly across your head toward the other side of your body (that's nine o'clock on the clock face) begin the turn.

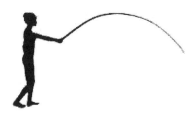

The Turn

Simply change the direction that your hand is rotating. It's important to keep your hand high, so that all the motion happens in the helicopter plane. Your palm should be facing down and your thumb should be pushing the handle back in the other direction.

A loop forms in the whip as the popper continues behind your back while the handle is moving in front of you. The crack should happen in front of you, a little toward the whip side.

The Follow Through

You can continue rotating the whip above your head in the opposite direction. You are now set up for a reverse overhead crack. Alternatively, after the crack has happened, you can allow your arm to slope downward so that the whip falls to the ground behind you.

What Went Wrong?

- *Indecision.* The usual sign of this is that the whip keeps rotating in the same direction above your head. Sometimes it will twitch a little, but then keep going round the same way. The cure for this is to make up your mind that you will always change direction on the second revolution. Sometimes counting the revolutions out loud can help: "One, two, crack!"
- *Too small a motion.* You should be making this motion with your whole arm, and not just spinning the whip with your wrist. While you can maintain a spin like this, it takes the whole of your arm to reverse it.
- *Leaving the helicopter plane.* It's important to keep the whip up above your head, rather than wrapped around it. Make sure that after the crack you can continue the rotation of the whip in the opposite direction, without taking the whip too far up or down. Later you may wish to tilt the plane of this crack for two-handed work, but for now I'd like you to keep it as level as possible.
- *Dan's crack.* My son Dan does the setup for an overhead crack, but then brings his arm straight back over his head vertically, converting the motion into a forward crack in the rear wall plane. The whip cracks to his whip side and a little behind him. It works for him, but I don't recommend it as there is less you can do with the follow through and it's harder to get a good crack, as you are changing planes.

Next Steps

Once you are comfortable with the basic cracks you can start to explore their variations. The next three chapters deal with the ways that you can progress into more complicated versions of each of the basic cracks. Within each chapter the material is arranged in a good order to learn, but feel free to skip around from chapter to chapter if you want to work on improving your overhead or sidearm repertoire at the same time as you progress with the forward crack.

Chapter Five
Forward Crack Variations

The Rotating Forward Crack

This is a fun and easy way to fire off a whole series of cracks in quick succession. When you finish a forward crack, the whip should be lying in a line straight ahead of you. Turn your body 180 degrees. The whip is now in a line behind you, and you are ready to do another forward crack. You should be turning from the whip side toward the other side of your body so that the whip does not wrap around you.

Soon you will be able to crack and turn, crack and turn, smoothly and continuously until you get dizzy. I like to take a step forward with my whip side foot as I crack, then pivot on both feet so that my whip side foot is ready to take another step forward. Keep the whip moving smoothly from the follow through of one crack into the setup of the next. Make sure it keeps moving in a plane, even though your body is turning during the transition.

The Inward Sideways Crack

This is almost the same arm motion as the forward crack. However, your body is turned 90 degrees towards your whip side, so that the crack takes place in the front wall plane rather than the shoulder wall plane. I found it quite scary the first time I tried it, as the whip was whizzing by a few inches in front of my face, but if you are comfortable with the forward crack it will very quickly feel natural.

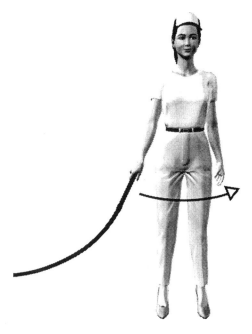

Start with the whip extended to your whip side in the front wall plane. The palm of your hand should also be in the front wall plane, facing your body.

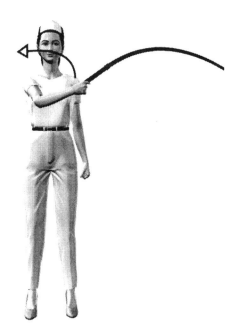

Bring your hand and arm up in front of you to the other side of your body, with your forearm staying in the front wall plane.

Allow your wrist and elbow to bend, so that the whip swings up and over to the whip side of your body again. Don't let your elbow swing forward, keep it pointing to the other side of your body.

The Turn

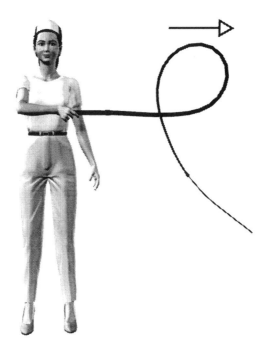

Bring your arm back down to the other side of your body, straightening your elbow and your wrist.

The Follow Through

Leave your arm extended and allow the whip to fall to the floor pointing to the other side of your body.

What Went Wrong?

- *All the usual stuff.* Since this is a forward crack in another plane, you will find yourself reinventing all the problems that you had with the forward crack. The most popular problems are below. If you find that you're hitting yourself on a regular basis you're probably suffering from one of these.

- *That elbow again.* The elbow swings up across the front of your body and back down again. It does not move to point forward as you are about to begin the turn. That's just a bad habit you picked up as a kid playing baseball or rounders. It serves you right for spending all that time on ball games when you could have been cracking whips.

- *Waving the handle.* Once again, you need to keep the handle tilted just far enough away from your body that the whip clears your hand. A lot of people seem to feel the urge to let the handle tilt backwards when it is above their head. Tennis players, maybe? Get someone to watch you from the side and see if you are doing this.

The Outward Sideways Crack

I used to teach this move after the reverse crack, but one of my students pointed out that I was doing it the wrong way around. This is actually an easier way to learn the reverse crack motion, and while it may feel a little awkward at first, it does not feel nearly as awkward as the reverse crack, so now I teach this one first. It's a very similar motion to the inward sideways crack, but your arm is pointing in the other direction and the whip is on the other side of your arm.

The Setup

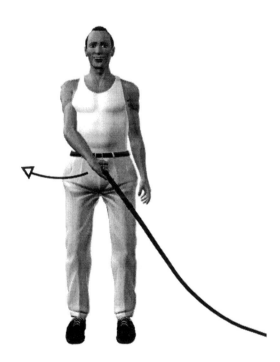

Start with the whip extended in the front wall plane, pointing toward the other side of your body. The whip in this picture is not on the ground, because it has just completed an inward sideways crack (more of that later) but you can just as easily start with the whip on the floor. Your palm should be in the front wall plane, facing away from you, and it will stay facing away from you. Imagine that you have a window right in front of you and you are polishing the glass with a cloth held in the palm of your hand, making a big sweeping motion on the whip side of your body. If you like you can come and practice on the windows at my house.

Swing the whip out to the whip side of your body, and then back over the top until it is pointing to the other side, all the while keeping it in the front wall plane.

The Turn

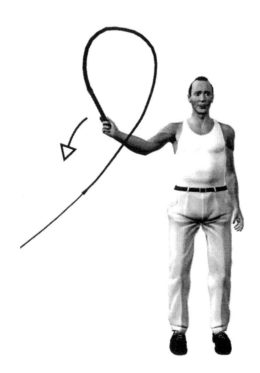

Bring your arm back down to the whip side of your body, straightening your elbow and wrist.

The Follow Through

Extend your arm, and allow the whip to fall to the floor on the whip side.

What Went Wrong?

- *More of the same.* You will find that this has all the problems of the forward and inward sideways cracks, with the added fun of hitting yourself on the side of the face if you get things wrong. Now would be a good time to wear a cowboy hat and a bad time to forget your eye protection.

The Reverse Crack

This is just the outward sideways crack twisted around so that it goes behind you instead of out to the side. It may feel quite awkward at first, but it will soon come to feel natural. Like the forward crack, the whole of this crack takes place in the shoulder wall plane.

The Setup

Take the knot in the palm of your hand, with your thumb pointing down the handle. Hold your arm down and a little forward. Arrange the whip so that it is lying in a line directly in front of you. Twist your arm, so that your elbow points towards your body and your palm faces outwards, with your thumb to the rear of the handle.

Swing your arm backward, keeping it in the shoulder wall plane. It's important to keep the palm of your hand facing away from you. Remember that window cleaning motion from the outward sideways crack? This time the window is in the shoulder wall plane.

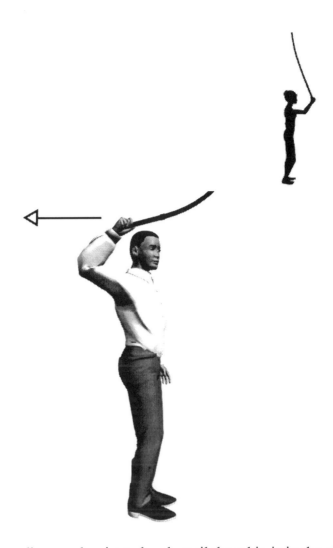

As the whip comes up, allow your elbow and wrist to bend, until the whip is in the air in front of you at head height.

The Turn

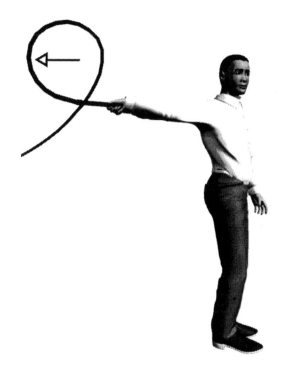

Straighten your elbow and then your wrist, so that your arm is pointing horizontally behind you. A loop will form in the whip, which will travel backward. The crack should happen well behind you in the shoulder wall plane, a little above head height.

The Follow Through

Keep your arm pointing backward until the whip cracks, and then continue downward. The whip should fall to the ground in a line behind you.

What Went Wrong?

This crack can suffer from all the problems of the forward crack, especially our old friend, inappropriate elbow motion. It is even more difficult to stay in the shoulder wall plane when your arm is twisted behind you. I'm not as flexible as I should be, so my reverse cracks happen somewhere on the outside of the shoulder wall plane, as I can't get my arm far enough back. I also twist my shoulders to help, but I try to make sure that I don't move my feet or my hips.

The Easy Windscreen Wiper

There's a much more difficult move that the Aussies call the windscreen wiper, which involves two stock whips doing volley cracks, but here's a couple of easy moves which give you a continuous series of cracks with one whip, and is a first step on the way to the Aussie version.

You alternate the inward and outward sideways cracks to make the whip travel backward and forward in front of you like a windscreen wiper. When you have completed an inward sideways crack, the whip is in the initial position for an outward sideways crack, and when you have finished that, the whip is perfectly positioned to do another inward sideways crack. The follow through from one crack becomes the setup of the next, and with a little practice you can just keep on going.

There's an interesting variation on this that uses both hands. First, learn to do inward and outward sideways cracks with both your left and your right hand. Notice that at the end of the setup for the outward sideways crack for your right hand, the whip has the same position and motion as it does at the end of the setup for the inward sideways crack with your left hand.

It's possible to do the setup for the outward sideways crack with one hand and at the end of the setup transfer the whip handle to the other hand. Now do the turn and follow through for the inward forward crack for that hand, transition smoothly into the setup for the outward forward crack and transfer the whip back to the original hand. You can keep this up indefinitely. I always like the feel of continuous whip moves that use both sides of my body equally.

Figure Eights

Once you have mastered the forward and reverse cracks, it's easy to alternate one and the other, just as you do for the windscreen wiper. When you have completed a forward crack, the whip is in the initial position for a reverse crack, and when you have completed a reverse crack, the whip should be in the initial position for a forward crack. All you need to do for the transition is bring your arm down, and twist it so your palm faces in the opposite direction. By smoothly alternating forward and reverse cracks you can create a series of bangs that will be sure to impress all but the most phlegmatic of livestock.

The Downward Snap

I have some reservations about teaching this crack, because it is dangerous and bad for your whip. However, it is the only way I know to crack a long whip in a crowded room with a low ceiling, and I could never resist an impressive party trick.

The danger is because the point at which the whip cracks is very close to your face. If you get the move just a little wrong, you may seriously hurt yourself. Full-face protection is essential the first few times you try it. The wear on the whip is because you use the leverage of the handle far more than you usually would, and this puts an undue strain on the whip at the point where the handle joins the thong. Once you have learned this crack, save it for performance, and don't make an everyday habit of it. Or do it with a stock whip or a cow whip which are built to take more torque on the handle.

The Setup

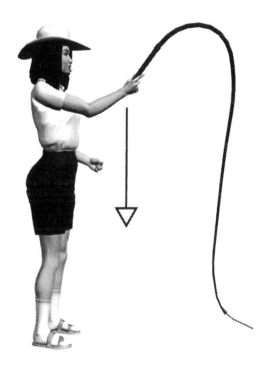

Extend your arm forward with the elbow slightly bent, and the whip handle pointing upward at 45 degrees in the shoulder wall plane. The thong will hang downward, and the fall should be on the floor directly below the thong. With a shorter whip it may help to start the whip moving upward by raising your hand before you go into the turn.

The Turn

Bring your hand and arm down as rapidly as you can, pointing the handle downward as you do so. The thong will double back on itself and crack just in front of you.

The Follow Through
Let your arm fall to your side, and the whip will land at your feet.

What Went Wrong?
- *Curved motion.* For this crack to work, the thong must double back on itself in a very tight U-shape. If you make a curved, sweeping motion with your hand rather than going straight downward, you will not get a crack and you may end up with a whip in your face.
- *Lopsided setup.* The fall, (and for a longer whip, some of the thong) should be on the floor directly below the rest of the whip. Make sure it is all in roughly the same spot and doesn't go off to one side, or this will make the crack a lot less predictable.

The Cheap Crack

This is an easy way to start a routine with a crack that your audience is not expecting. It works better with longer whips.

The Setup
Simply lay the whip out in front of you in the shoulder wall plane, holding the handle with your arm straight down as if you are about to do a forward crack. With a shorter whip you will get a louder crack if you begin by swinging your arm back, so the whip is sliding backward on the floor.

The Turn

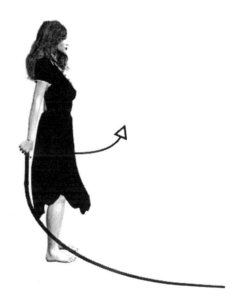

Keeping your arm straight, swing it forward and up as fast as you can.

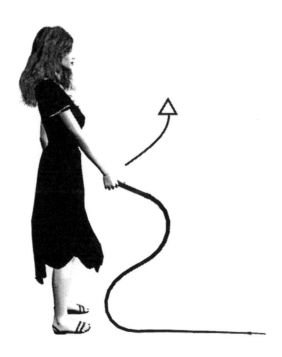

The whip will form an S-shape, which on a good day will give you two crisp little cracks, very close together.

The Follow Through
At this point you are in the setup for a forward crack, so just carry on and do one.

What Went Wrong?
- *Short whip.* This will work happily with an eight foot whip (2.4m) and will probably work with a six foot whip, but you will certainly have difficulty with anything shorter.
- *Rough surface.* If the whip drags on the surface then it is far less likely to crack. I haven't been able to get this to work very well on grass, but it is fine on a wooden stage or a carpeted floor.
- *Slow turn.* This is an easy crack, so if you are on a smooth surface and your whip is long enough and you are still having problems, you are probably just not moving your arm fast enough.

The Coachman's Crack

This crack works well with the long handled whips that might be used by the drivers of horse drawn carriages. The crack itself happens further back than a forward crack, so it is behind the horses, which encourages them to go forward. A crack in front of the horses might encourage them to rear up or do other nervous horsey things not conducive to forward motion of the carriage.

The coachman's crack will also work fine with shorter bullwhips, but if you want to do it with a ten foot whip you may have to stand on a chair. If your timing is a little off with this one, it can produce a thunderous crack right next to your ear, so you may want to have an ear plug in place.

The Setup
Start out just as if you are doing a forward crack, until your upper arm is horizontal and your forearm is vertical.

Wait. The whip carries on down behind you.

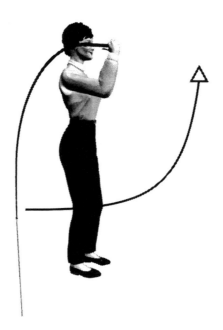

Wait. The whip scrapes the floor and is now coming up in front of you.

Wait. The fall and popper are now right in front of you again, on the way up.

If you did this right, the whip will be moving just fast enough to reach horizontal in front of you, but no further. When it is about to fall back it's time for the turn.

The Turn

Straighten out your arm and point your wrist forward, just as you would for the forward crack.

The Follow Through

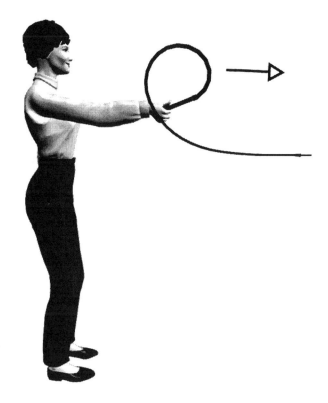

After the whip has cracked let your arm continue downward, just as for the forward crack.

What Went Wrong?

This crack suffers from all the problems of the forward crack, as well as a couple that are all its own.

- *Letting your elbow get up too high.* Don't let your elbow get up any higher than horizontal; it's fine to keep it a bit below that.
- *Not waiting long enough.* This crack seems to take longer than you can imagine. Make sure the popper is at head height in front of you before you start the turn.
- *Using too much force in the setup.* If the whip cracks behind you or right by your ear, it was probably still moving upward when you went into the turn. Make the setup a little gentler.

Chapter Six
Sidearm Crack Variations

The sidearm crack takes place in the belt plane on the whip side of the body. There are three closely related cracks that take place in the shoulder wall plane above and below your hand, and in the belt plane on the other side of your body.

The Overhand Crack

This is also called the forward flick. It is a useful crack for cutting targets under a low ceiling. Some performers who work in night clubs and cruise ships prefer this crack because it can be used on any stage, no matter how close to your head the lights are.

The Setup

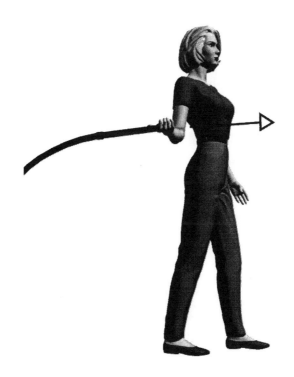

As with the sidearm crack, stand with the whip extended behind you. Your elbow should be bent with the palm of your hand facing upwards. Push your hand smartly forward and a little upward.

The Turn

As your arm extends, twist your wrist forward, so that the whip rolls over the top of your hand. A U-shape will form in the shoulder wall plane that will roll forward and crack.

The Follow Through

Hold your arm extended with the whip handle pointing forward. After the whip has cracked it will fall to the ground in front of you.

What Went Wrong?
- *Hitting the back of legs*. You probably did not have the whip in a straight line behind you before you started the crack.
- *Leaving the shoulder wall plane*. The U-shape you make with the whip should be entirely in a vertical plane. Don't let it slope at all.
- *Swinging*. Watch the U-shape as it rolls forward. It should be as narrow as possible. If it is wide, that is because you swung your hand in an arc rather than pushing the whip straight forward.

Using a Shorter Whip
This is a popular crack for short snake whips, too, but the setup is a little different. A long whip can be extended on the floor behind your hand. A short whip will dangle below your hand.

An easy way to fix this problem is to make the crack in the front wall plane, and use the other hand to hold the whip in the correct setup position.

A more elegant way to get the whip into the position you want, extended in the air directly behind you, is to first swing it backwards and up. Ideally you will judge the swing so that the whip is in a perfectly straight line exactly behind your hand with no upward or downward momentum as you start the crack. It's possible to go from the follow through straight into the swing that begins the next setup, thus providing a continuous rapid fire series of overhand cracks.

The Underhand

For the Aussies, this is the first part of a two-crack move called the whoosh-bang. I guess that makes it the whoosh. It's important to keep this crack in the shoulder wall plane, so that the follow through brings the whip past your face and not straight into it. Wear eye protection until you are very good at this one.

The Setup
Start just as for the forward crack, with the whip in a line on the floor, directly behind your whip hand.

Bring your hand up slightly, and straight forward, keeping it low. It may help you to take a step forward when you do this.

The Turn

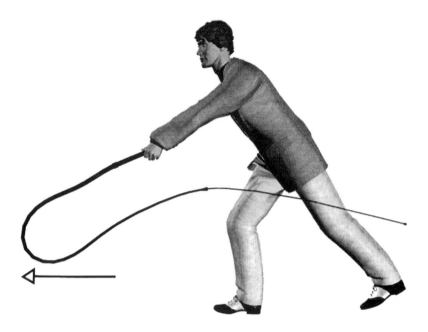

When your arm is fully extended forward and downward leave it there for a moment. The whip forms a U-shape in the shoulder wall plane, which will roll forward and crack.

The Follow Through

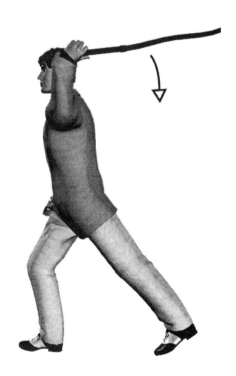

After the whip has cracked, bring your arm rapidly up and back, so that the whip comes back over your whip hand and falls to the floor again behind you.

What Went Wrong?

- *Carpet drag.* This crack works best on tile or wooden surfaces. During the setup, part of your whip will be dragging along the floor. If you are on grass or carpeting, the friction may slow it down so that it will not crack. You can compensate for this to some extent by lifting the whip at the start of the setup, but it will always work better on a smooth surface. Never try this crack on an abrasive surface such as sand or pavement. Generally it's very bad for a long whip to use it on such a surface.
- *Leaving the shoulder wall plane.* If the whip comes back and hits you in the face, it has clearly left the shoulder wall plane. Make sure that it is directly behind your whip hand when you start, and that your hand motion does not go to one side or the other.
- *Bringing your hand up too early.* If your U-shape is too wide the whip will not crack. Keeping your hand low after the initial lift will correct this.

The Reverse Underhand

The Setup

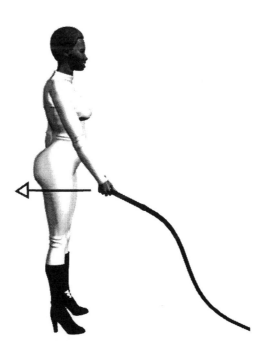

Start with your arm pointing forward and down, and the whip extended in a line on the floor in front of you. Bring your arm smartly backwards, pulling the whip along the floor.

The Turn

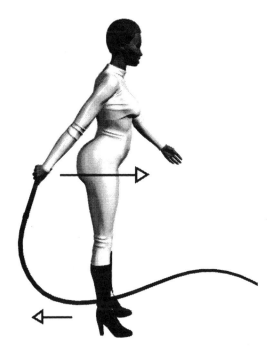

When the whip is passing underneath your hand, reverse the direction of your arm, and bring your hand forward again.

The Follow Through

Let your arm return to its starting position, and the whip will crack just behind you, and come back past your shoulder to land back in front of you.

Alternative Follow Through

For comic effect, as the whip cracks, thrust your hips forward, yelp and grab your bottom. I can only speculate why audiences find this entertaining. If you want to live dangerously, you can also try doing this crack between your legs rather than by your side. It's another crowd pleaser, which just goes to show that the average audience contains a lot of sick minds.

What Went Wrong?

This crack can suffer from the same problems as the underhand crack, particularly *carpet drag*. However, if you *leave the shoulder wall plane*, you only risk hitting yourself on the back rather than in the face.

The Backhand

For this crack we are back in the belt plane. I like to alternate it with the sidearm, taking a step forward with each crack. My ambition is to make this motion as graceful as a Tai Chi form, but I still have a long way to go.

The Setup

Start with the whip in a line directly behind you on the other side of your body. Your whip side arm should be extended across the front of your body, with the palm of the hand facing downward, and your thumb pointing along the whip handle backwards.

Lift your whip hand a little and push it forward. Make sure it goes in a straight line, and does not swing across the front of your body.

The Turn

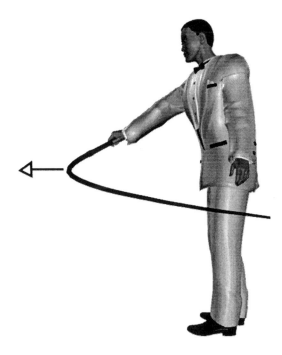

   As the whip travels past your hand, straighten your wrist, allowing the usual U-shape to form in the whip. Keep your arm extended forward until the whip cracks.

The Follow Through

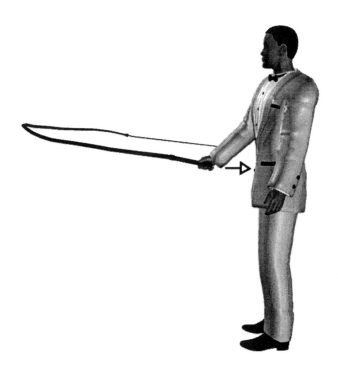

Gently guide the whip back on the whip side of your body. It should end up positioned to begin the sidearm crack.

What Went Wrong?

This crack can suffer from the same problems as the sidearm crack. Watch that U-shape as it rolls forward and make sure it is good and narrow.

Chapter Seven
Overhead Crack Variations

Reverse Overhead

Remember how with the overhead crack, you changed the direction of a whip rotating in the helicopter plane? Now it's time to switch directions again, and get it going round the way it was when you started out. It's great fun to alternate these two cracks, with one or two overhead revolutions of the whip between each crack.

The Setup

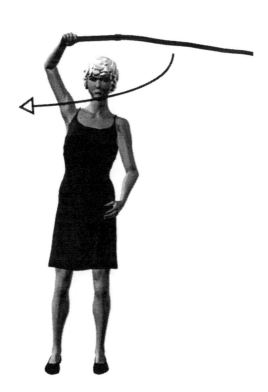

I usually use an overhead crack as the setup for this, but you can start with the whip on the floor. In either case, you want the whip rotating over your head in the helicopter plane, in the opposite direction to the setup of the overhead crack. Remember to make a big motion using as much of your arm as possible, and not just your wrist.

When your whip arm is pointing directly away from your body sideways and upwards, change the direction of the rotation. Bring your arm back across in front of your body, keeping your hand well up in the air. A loop will form in the whip behind you and roll across your head to crack in front of you on the other side of your body.

The Follow Through
Keep the whip rotating in the helicopter plane.

Hungarian Pig Drover's Crack

I learned this crack at the 1994 International Jugglers' Association annual festival in Burlington, Vermont. The person who taught me didn't give me a name for it, but he did say that he had learned it from a Hungarian pig drover. I called it "The Hungarian Pig Drover's Crack" in the Bullwhip FAQ, and the name seems to have stuck. It's certainly not unique to Hungary, and I doubt if all the pig drovers there can do it, just one particular pig drover.

It takes a little practice to get the timing for this crack just right, but is very satisfying when you do. It's a little easier with stock whips and cow whips, so if you have one available you might want to learn with that and transfer the skill to a bullwhip later. It's easier with longer whips. Remember to wear eye protection, as the crack happens right in front of your face.

The Setup
Start with the whip rotating in the helicopter plane, just as for the overhead crack.

The Turn

When your whip hand is pointing sideways away from your body, stop the motion of your arm suddenly, but allow the whip to continue to rotate.

When it has made a quarter revolution, start moving your hand rapidly to catch up. Make sure you follow the line of the whip in the air, and catch up as fast as you can. You should now have an S-shaped curve rolling down the whip. With a little luck you will get two cracks close together, one from each bend of the S. However, you can count it as a success if you get just one crack.

The Follow Through

Continue with the rotation in the helicopter plane. Unlike the overhead crack you have not changed direction, so you can repeat this crack as often as you like with a couple of revolutions in between. When you get better, try doing it on every revolution. It's a bit hectic, but quite impressive if you can nail it. There's also a version that goes in the opposite direction. See if you can work that one out without my help.

What Went Wrong?

- *Not waiting long enough.* Make sure the popper of the whip is right in front of you before you start your hand moving again.
- *Leaving the helicopter plane.* If you wait too long, or you are not swinging the whip fast enough to begin with, the whip will drop out of the helicopter plane, and won't crack. If the whip hits you, this is a sure sign that it has left the helicopter plane!

Switching Hands

Now I've thoroughly impressed on you the importance of keeping overhead cracks in the helicopter plane, I'd like to teach you a couple of tricks where this isn't true. Imagine that the helicopter plane is tilted at about 30 degrees from the horizontal so that it slopes down on the whip side of your body and up on the other side. This is the plane where this crack takes place. It feels like a hybrid between the forward crack and the overhead crack. Since you will be alternating hands, you should be able to do both of those cracks using either hand before you try this one.

The Setup

Start with the whip extended behind you on the floor.

Bring your arm forward and upward, so that the whip swings up in front of you. Allow your elbow and wrist to bend so that the whip is extended backward over your other shoulder.

The Turn

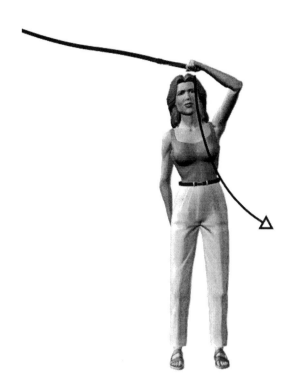

Now take your arm back the way it came. The loop in the whip should roll over your whip side shoulder and crack in front of you

The Follow Through

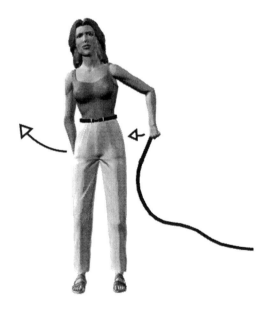

Swing the whip back behind you.

The Continuation

Place the handle in the other hand behind your back. You can now repeat the move on the opposite side of your body.

What Went Wrong?

- *Changing planes.* The most common problem with this crack and the next one is that people will try to do the setup in one plane, and then change to a different plane for the turn and follow through. I like to visualize the planes by imagining that I am standing in a tent with a sloping roof on each side of me, and I have to keep all the motion of the whip touching the roof of the tent.

Alternating With Two Whips

For this move you will need two whips of about the same length and weight. If you plan on doing a lot of two-handed work you may want to ask your favorite whip maker to make you a matched pair. Two whips braided by the same person at the same time can be made more nearly identical than whips produced at different times, as the craftsman can use the same hide, and compare them as they are made to make sure that they are weighted, balanced and tapered the same.

This crack is exactly the same as the last one, except that instead of passing one whip from hand to hand, you use a whip in each hand. It also goes a little faster. As one whip is at the turn, the other is beginning its setup. Let your shoulders swing from side to side, and if you like, take a step forward with every crack. Make sure that all the motion of the whips is in those sloping planes I mentioned above.

Chapter Eight
Volleys

Volleys are a very rapid series of cracks where the whip doubles back on itself after every crack. It is easiest with bullwhips in the six to eight foot (1.8m to 2.4m) range. I think it's easier to volley stock whips, as the long handle makes the rapid backward and forward action more natural. As I write this my friend Robert Dante holds the Guinness world record for being the fastest bullwhip cracker in the world for making 214 volley cracks in one minute with a six foot bullwhip. By the time this book is in print that record may well have been broken, and if not, well, I'll leave that up to you.

Warming Up

This is quite a difficult trick, because there is very little time between one crack and the next, so if any errors creep into the motion of the whip it is hard to correct them, and they grow bigger with each crack. Pretty soon the whip has stopped cracking, and if you keep on trying to volley it may start hitting. Rather than starting straight into the volley action, I think it's best to work up to it with some simpler moves that will teach you the necessary control in small increments.

First, kneel down on the floor, sitting on your heels. Lay the whip out in a line behind you in the shoulder wall plane, holding it as if you are about to go into the turn on the forward crack. Now, bring your hand gently over in an overhand crack motion, so that the whip rolls over your hand and lands on the floor in front of you. You are trying to get it to end up in a perfect straight line in the shoulder wall plane. Now reverse the hand motion, and try to get the whip to roll out in a line behind you. Repeat this until you can get the whip to roll out straight every time.

You'll find that to get this working smoothly, it's best to have your elbow away from your body on the whip side. "But Andrew," you say, "What about all that time I spent learning to keep my elbow forward? Now you're telling me it should be sideways! I'm confused." Yes, dear reader, I must admit I was confused, too, when I made a video of myself volleying and watched it in slow motion to prepare the illustrations for this book. There was my elbow out to the side. I even went and checked a video of Robert Dante volleying just to make sure I was doing it right. His elbow was out to the side, too.

The important thing, though, is that once your elbow is out to the side, it stays there, and does not flail around. Your upper arm should not move very much when you are volleying, all the motion is in the forearm and the wrist.

Once you have got the whip rolling out straight in both directions, all you have to do is speed up the motion and stand up, and you will be volleying… If only it were that easy! Here's another exercise that will help you sneak up on volleying. Make sure that your figure eights are completely solid, both in the front wall plane and the shoulder wall plane. Now you are ready to move on to fast figure eights.

Fast Figure Eights

The Setup
Do a forward crack using your forearm, with your elbow out to the whip side. Don't follow through.

The Turn
Instead, just before the whip cracks, pull your forearm back and bend your wrist. (See the first picture in the description of volleys on the following pages.) The whip should crack in front of you and then flick back behind you and crack.

The Follow Through
Let your hand go back behind you, down and forward. You are now in the setup for a forward crack. Repeat the whole sequence as many times as you like.

The result of all this should be a crack-crack-pause-crack-crack-pause rhythm. While you are working on this, you should also be working on reverse fast figure eights.

Reverse Fast Figure Eights

The Setup
Do a reverse crack, but don't follow through.

The Turn
Instead pull your forearm forward and bend your wrist. (See the third picture in the description of volleys on the following pages.) The whip should flick back in front of you and crack.

The Follow Through
Let your hand go in front of you, down and backward. You are now in the setup for a reverse crack. Repeat the whole sequence as many times as you like.

Adding Volley Cracks

That second crack in the fast figure eight patterns is a single volley crack. Once you have both directions down, you can start to put them together. However, you'll still have difficulties if you try to go straight into the volley pattern. Instead, you should try to add one extra volley crack into the fast figure eights. To do this, you start the fast figure eight move as usual, but right after you have completed the turn, take your arm back forward again. After it cracks behind you, the whip should flick forward and crack in front of you.

You can now follow through into the setup for a reverse crack. You can probably guess what is coming next. After the reverse crack, do two more volley cracks, and follow through into a forward crack. You can keep this up indefinitely. The follow through and setup motion gives you time to correct any errors that have crept into the motion of the whip during the volley cracks.

When you can do two volley cracks in a row in a figure eight pattern, try three. Do a forward crack, pull the whip back for a crack behind you, just before it cracks send it forward again, and just before it cracks in front of you pull it back again. Now follow through behind you, down, and up in front of you, and repeat the process.

When you're nailing that one go for four volley cracks, and when that is getting comfortable, it's time to start working on continuous volleys.

Volleys At Last

If you've worked through all those exercises, you should have a pretty good idea of how to do continuous volleys, but let's go over it one more time, with pictures.

The Setup

I usually start with a forward crack, but you can start with an overhand if you prefer. In either case, don't follow through after the crack.

The Turn

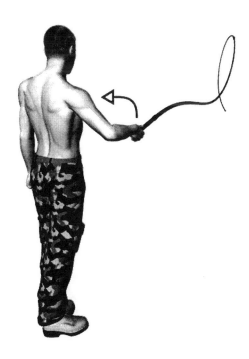

Instead, bring your hand and arm back.

The whip doubles back and cracks behind you.

The Turn

Yes, that's right, since we are cracking continuously there is no follow through, only another turn. As the whip is cracking behind you bring your arm forward again.

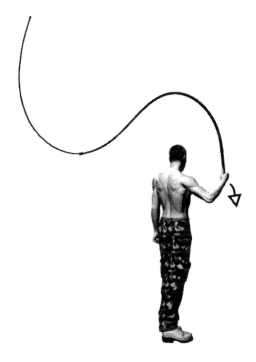

The whip doubles back and cracks in front of you.

The Turn

And keep on going backward and forward until you get tired or bored, or mess up (which is what usually happens to me).

What Went Wrong?

- *Leaving the shoulder wall plane.* It's really important the keep the motion of the whip as close to a perfect plane as you can. As usual, make sure that you are not wiggling your elbow from side to side, or changing the angle at which you are tilting the handle relative to the shoulder wall plane.
- *Timing.* Every whip has its own speed at which it will volley best. Experiment with going faster and slower, especially slower. Every time you pick up a new whip and volley with it, let it teach you the right speed.

What's Next?

When you have learned to volley with one hand, go back and try with the other. When you have that working, try both hands at once. Experiment with different timings. You can move your hands together, or in opposite directions, or have one following the other half a beat behind. Try volleying with your whip hand on the other side of your body. Now change from one side to the other while still volleying. When you can do that in either direction, change sides every time the whip cracks in front of you. Now do that with both hands at the same time, without tangling your whips. Congratulations, you've just learned the arrowhead, a trick difficult enough to be one of the ten routines you would need to enter an Australian whip cracking championship. Those guys are good!

Chapter Nine
Cutting Targets

Once you start to practice with a bullwhip, sooner or later someone will ask you if you can knock a cigarette out of his or her mouth with it. Of course you can. Arrange them carefully a few feet in front of you, ask them if they have medical insurance, crack the whip well away from them and then run over and whack the cigarette out of their mouth with the handle!

Of course, it is possible to get accurate enough with a whip to do this trick for real, but don't expect to get there quickly. Generally a shorter whip is more accurate than a longer one. Bullwhips with longer canes extending further into the thong are sometimes called *target whips*, because the longer cane also makes them more accurate.

Cracks to Use

Generally the target you want to cut is held horizontally, so to cut it the whip should be moving in a vertical plane. The forward crack and the overhand crack are the best for this. For me the forward crack is the more accurate, but that's probably because I practice it more. The overhand crack has the advantage that it will work under a low ceiling, so if you will be working mostly indoors you may prefer to concentrate on that.

You do not want to have the whip crack right on the target. Aim to have it crack a couple of feet (0.6m) higher, so that the follow through of the popper or fall does the cutting. That way when you have an assistant holding the target, that one in a thousand times when you mess up will not require a trip to the emergency room, just an ice pack and an apology. If you wet the end of the popper you can see the exact spot it cracks from the puff of microscopic water droplets it gives off.

Since you are aiming for consistency, make sure that all the things that you can control easily are the same every time. Your posture and stance, your distance from the target, and the initial position of the whip should be identical for every crack. It's really important that the whip travel in a perfect vertical plane. You have a lot less control if you're trying to cut a target with a diagonal stroke.

Practice Targets

Accurate targeting takes a lot of practice, and when you begin, you will want something you can aim for which will show you where your whip is landing, without damaging the whip or needing to be set up again after each crack.

One solution is to use a horizontal rod with a number of rings on it close together. Shower curtain rings on a broom handle, held in place with a couple of nails, will work fine. There should be a little slack between the rings so that each one can turn independently of the others. Now, lay the broom handle across a couple of chair backs and aim for the center of the row of rings. You will be able to see how close you came by watching which ring is spinning afterwards.

Another possibility is to get some large cardboard boxes and stack them up in two piles about five feet (1.5m) high so that there is a gap of about a foot (0.3m) between them. Now try cracking the whip so that the follow through takes it down between the two stacks without touching either side. Once that is easy, move the boxes closer and closer together, and see how small you can make the gap.

If all this seems like too much work, you can always try trimming a handy bush, one leaf at a time.

Hand Held Targets

When you can hit within an inch (2.5cm) of the point you are aiming at every single time, you are ready to graduate to a target held by an assistant. Don't go straight for the cigarette in the mouth, however. Start with a length of spaghetti held in a hand clad in a leather gauntlet. It gives me great satisfaction to whack away at a packet of organic whole-wheat pasta abandoned in my kitchen by a militant vegetarian houseguest, as it certainly isn't good for anything else. It's also biodegradable and edible, so you can use it in the park without worrying about the litter you are creating. The squirrels will be happy to clean up for you.

Some experts say that you should always try to hit the target with the popper so that you get a clean cut, while others say that you should cut with the fall, especially for hand held targets, as it will do less damage to your assistant should you happen to miss. Personally I vote for safety over style, and make sure that my targets are fragile enough that I don't have to use the popper.

If you want to perform this trick in front of a large audience, spaghetti is not very visible. Instead, you can save those polystyrene packages that you buy meat and produce in at the supermarket, and cut them into strips about half an inch (1cm) wide. To make sure that they break cleanly, you can gimmick them by cutting them half way through in the middle with a sharp knife.

Other targets I've seen used include flowers (sometimes an artificial flower stuck into a drinking straw so the whip knocks the flower out of the end of the straw, and sometimes real flowers), and hollow tubular pasta which has been filled with baby powder and sealed. This gives a nice visual puff when it is broken.

Another good stunt for performance is to have an assistant stand facing you, holding up a sheet of newspaper by the corners at arms' length. Use the whip to cut the newspaper in half. Your assistant can help by pulling apart on the corners. They then take one of the pieces and hold that up for you to cut in half again. Depending on how accurate you are, you can work down to a piece that is postcard sized or smaller. Since your assistant is standing directly in front of the cracking whip you don't want to get too close. It's a good idea to start well out of range, and then move a little closer with every crack, until you are just hitting the paper.

Holding Your Own

If you don't have an assistant to hold your target, you can hold your own. Anywhere you place a target so that it intersects the shoulder wall plane, it will be hit by some part of a whip during a forward crack. If you have a fragile enough target, you don't need to hit it with a fast moving fall or cracker, letting the thong tap it as it goes by will work just as well, and the audience will not know the difference. (Shhh... Don't show them this book.) Try doing a forward crack while holding a target in your other hand, just in front of your whip side shoulder. Keep doing forward cracks as you edge the target out towards the whip side, and pretty soon you will be hitting it with the whip.

You can hold a target with your other hand in several different positions. Try it behind your back, behind your head or under your whip arm. You can also cut a target held in your own mouth, either by turning your head to the side and using a forward crack, or facing forward and doing an inward sideways crack. If you hold a target on top of your head, pointing straight up through the helicopter plane, you can cut it with an overhead crack.

Popping Balloons

Cracking a whip so that it punctures a balloon creates a nice showy effect, especially if you put a little baby powder in the balloon before you inflate it so that it pops in a cloud of smoke. However, latex is tough stuff, and to pop a balloon you need the crack to happen precisely at the surface of the balloon, which can be difficult to achieve. Following through with the fall or popper will not pop a balloon, though it will work for other targets. I've found that nylon whips work better than leather for this as the fall is more abrasive, and that it really helps to have a fully inflated balloon.

If you would like to perform this trick, but don't want to put in the many hours of practice necessary to perfect it, there are a couple of ways you can fake it. One is to use an assistant to hold the balloon. The assistant has a thumbtack taped to a thumb. As you crack the whip in roughly the direction of your assistant, they pop the balloon with the thumbtack.

You can also have the balloon on a stand which has a point, or resting on an abrasive surface. That way the impact of the whip will press it onto something else which then pops it. That's show business!

Snuffing Candles

If your popper passes close enough to a candle flame, the draft created will blow it out, especially if you use a big, fluffy popper. Even the follow through can snuff a flame, so this trick is easier than popping balloons. I haven't worked on it much but it seems as if it is best to crack just in front of the candle so that you don't knock it over. The forward crack or any of the sidearm crack variants will work. You can turn this into a game — score one point for every time you put the candle out, subtract one point for every time you knock it over, ten points for getting candle wax on your carpet and a hundred points for setting fire to your house.

You can also try flicking a light switch on and off with alternating underhand and overhand cracks, or even work on the trick performed by English whip maestro Vince Bruce. He throws a playing card into the air with his left hand and before it hits the ground slices it in half with a whip held in his right.

Chapter Ten
Wraps

After a whip has cracked, most of its energy is expended, and the follow through can be used to wrap around a person or object without doing any damage. This is a popular stunt in movies, where the whip-wielding hero may wrap a gun hand to disarm the villain, or wrap a tree branch to swing to safety. There are also some beautiful moves where the whip wraps around the person who cracked it.

The longer the whip, the safer the wrap, as the crack is further away from the target. I use a twelve-foot whip for wrapping people.

Wrapping People

Use the sidearm crack, and practice on a smooth upright pole. A six-foot post driven into the ground will do. (Trees are usually too rough and will abrade the whip when you pull it to unwrap it.) With a twelve-foot whip the target should be about eight to ten feet away from you, so that all of the fall and popper and some of the thong wrap around it after the crack. Aim the whip a little to the whip side of the target, and the follow through will naturally make it wrap. A little shake of the handle and a gentle pull is usually enough to unwrap it.

Mark your target with colored electrical tape at different heights, and aim for each maker in turn. You should be able to wrap within a few inches of any marker you like before you try this on a person. When you can wrap the target in your chosen spot on every attempt you can substitute a well-padded person for the pole. Aim for about waist height, and when you have that down you can aim for spots higher and lower. It is dangerous to try to wrap someone above chest height!

When you have wrapped a person, a firm pull on the whip will spin them around as they are pulled towards you. The whole sequence has an interesting psychological effect on your assistant. First they get to watch a long whip rolling towards them at ever increasing speed. There is a loud crack and the whip wraps around their body, miraculously, as it seems to them, without hurting them. Then, just when they think the worst is over, they are pulled off balance and spun around!

Wrapping Horizontal Objects

To wrap a railing or an outstretched arm, use an overhand crack aimed above your target. As with the previous move, practice your accuracy with inanimate objects before you graduate to well-padded people.

Locking a Wrap

Remember that oft repeated movie scene where the hero wraps a tree branch or balcony, swings to safety kicking over half a dozen stuntmen and then with a deft flick of the wrist unhooks his whip to use it in the next scene? I haven't actually tried this stunt myself, as I can't afford the stuntmen, but here's how it might be done.

First of all, make sure that your whip will take your weight. The whip used for swinging from in *The Mask of Zorro* had a steel cable core, and the chances are that yours does not. So, tie the fall to a branch using a knot that will untie easily, and put all your weight on the handle. Bounce up and down a bit, to try to break the fall. This treatment is not very good for your whip, by the way, but that never seems to worry Indiana Jones. It will certainly shorten your whip's life, but let's hope it will last all the way to the end of your next swing.

Assuming your fall hasn't broken, you next need to learn how to angle the overhand crack up in the air at 45 degrees or more. This is not very hard, if you are already good at the overhand crack. With a little practice you should be able to wrap an overhanging branch quite easily. At this point you will discover one of two things. Either the whip does not grip the branch tightly enough to support your weight, or it becomes so tightly wrapped around that after your magnificent swing across the abyss of doom, you have to go back and climb the tree to retrieve it.

However, with just the right branch and whip and a little luck you can lock the wrap in place and unlock it later. First the branch should be wrapped several times.

Usually the wrap will spiral in one direction along it.

Give the whip a little sideways flick towards the spiral so that the loop nearest you ends up overlapping one or more of the others. It should now support your weight if you keep tension on it. After you swing from it you should be able to get it to unwind by flicking it the other way and shaking gently.

Good luck, and remember, falling into a bottomless pit is not that bad. The real problem are those pits where you hit the bottom.

Wrapping Yourself

An elegant way to end a crack or sequence of cracks is to have the whip coil around your own body. You can do this from any crack where the follow through gives the whip some sideways momentum.

Let's assume you have just done an overhead crack, and the whip is travelling in front of you from the other side to the whip side.

Bring the whip handle down so that it rests on your whip side shoulder. As the whip continues behind your back, raise your other arm.

The whip will wrap around your other armpit. Lean your body towards the whip side, so that it continues to wrap around your neck on the whip side. If it comes around too low, you can use your whip handle as a sort of ramp to slide it up into the correct place.

Depending on the length of your whip you can repeat this two or three more times, so that the whip ends neatly coiled over your whip side shoulder and under the other arm. You can help the whip along a little by rocking your upper body, as if you are spinning a hula-hoop around your neck.

Wrap and Unwrap

I think this is the most elegant of follow throughs. Performer Brian Chic tells me that he invented it when he was a kid. Thanks, Brian! Between one crack and the next, the whip seems to glide around your body several times in sinuous curves. Again, you need to begin this move with a crack that gives some sideways momentum to the whip. Let's assume this time you start with a sidearm crack.

Follow through by bringing your whip handle up to your shoulder on the other side. Left to itself now, the whip would wrap itself in a helix down your body. However, you're not going to let it.

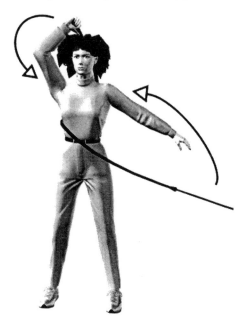

Start unwrapping the whip from the top by rotating the handle over your head, as the rest of the whip wraps. Try to keep as little of the whip as possible in contact with your body. When you are completely unwrapped the whip is rotating in the right direction for an overhead crack, if you just lift it up a bit. Of course, you can go into this move from an overhead crack as well, with the wrap and unwrap working in the other direction.

Chapter Eleven
Tricks and Stunts

Combinations

Sidearm to Overhead to Reverse to Forward

When you have mastered several basic cracks, you can try stringing them together into a sequence. Here's an example I like.

- From the sidearm crack follow though into a rotation above your head.
- Do an overhead crack, but instead of the usual follow through bring the whip down into the whip side shoulder wall plane.
- Do a reverse crack with the usual follow through.
- Finish with a forward crack.

Fargo Flash

In 1858 the Overland Mail Company (founded by Wells Fargo and other companies) began the first stagecoach service from St. Louis to San Francisco. The twice-weekly run took 25 days to travel the 2,757 miles. Arrival in San Francisco was an event, as the coach and team came in at a gallop. Waterman L. Ormsby, a passenger on the first stage, wrote, "Soon we struck the pavements, and with a whip, crack, and bound, shot through the streets to our destination, to the great consternation of everything in the way and to the little surprise of everybody."

In fact, the stagecoach drivers were sometimes referred to as "whips." It was a skilled, dangerous, and glamorous job. Amongst the whips working for Wells Fargo were Buffalo Bill Cody, Wyatt Earp, and Wild Bill Hickock. Another whip, Charley Parkhurst, was only discovered by the public to be a woman after her death. She is the first woman known to have voted in a U.S. election, many years before the suffragettes.

The story goes that the "whips" made use of the Fargo Flash to get a team of six horses moving, one crack for each horse.

Begin with a forward crack, but instead of following through downward, bring your whip hand back up and to the other side of your body a little, so that the whip comes back toward you, and passes by the other side of your head. Make sure it doesn't come back in your face, though.

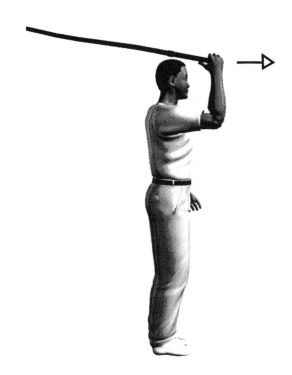

Let your wrist bend backward until the whip is right behind you in the air, then start your hand moving forward again, like the turn of a forward crack.

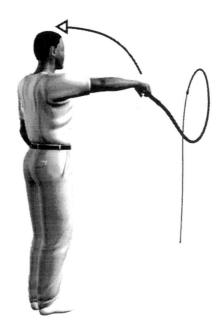

Extend your arm forward for the whip to crack again. Repeat once for each horse. It's possible to get the whip to crack on the backstroke as well as the forward stroke, but I don't think that would be much fun for the passengers in the stagecoach.

Queensland Flash and Sydney Flash

There is a story to these combinations, too. When you are herding cattle on horseback, and you have to motivate a difficult animal, you use three cracks, one in front to get the attention of the bull, one behind to get your horse moving, and then a loud one in front to get the bull moving. However, it's pretty much up to you which three cracks you use, so long as you get the story right! Forward crack, reverse crack, and then forward crack again will work fine, or overhand, reverse, overhead.

Aussie whip maker Mike Murphy says that if you go overhand crack, reverse volley crack, forward crack, that is a Sydney Flash, and if you go forward crack, reverse volley crack, forward crack, that's a Queensland Flash. If you've been working on fast figure eights, you'll see that a Queensland Flash is one and a half cycles of a fast figure eight. Feel free to make up your own flash and name it after the town you come from. If you want a laugh, ask me to show you the San Francisco skip.

Make Up Your Own

Don't just copy these sequences. Have fun making up your own. Once you have learned the basic moves, see how you can string them together and make variations on them. Remember that each crack should be in its own plane, and you should only change planes during the follow through. Can you put together cracks that are timed to music or that tell a story?

Pickups

You can pick up a whip lying on the ground by yanking the fall so that the handle flies towards you and you catch it and go straight into a crack. This is an impressive and fairly easy trick, especially with a longer whip. You can also use this move to snatch a whip out of the hand of an assistant, and then wrap them with the whip they were holding a moment ago.

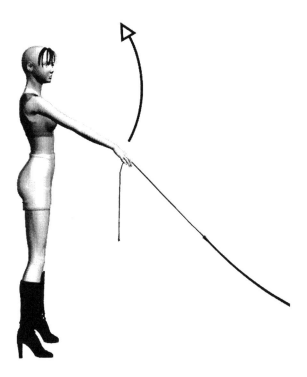

Start with the whip extended on the ground in a straight line in front of you in the whip side shoulder wall plane, with the handle furthest away from you. Grasp the knot that joins the fall to the popper.

Keeping your elbow straight, swiftly swing your arm up in the shoulder wall plane until it is pointing straight up. Now let go of the whip.

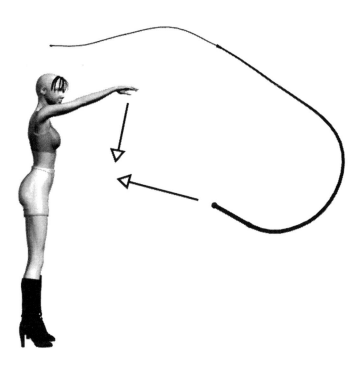

The handle should be flying toward you. It will have turned around so that it is coming at you knot first. Bring your hand down and catch the handle as it goes by.

Let your hand go back and the whip should also go back behind you. If you caught the middle of the handle rather than the knot, you can relax your grip a little and let motion of the whip slide the handle into the correct position. From here you can go easily into a sidearm crack or a reverse crack, or turn your body 180 degrees and do a forward crack.

If you are working with an assistant, they should grasp the handle very gently, and you can pull the whip out of their hand using the same motion. Take a large step or two towards them before you do the sidearm crack so that the whip will wrap around them rather than hitting them with the popper.

Throws and Catches

I think the first great whip-cracking act I ever saw was Joyce Rice. She's an ex-baton twirler, who works with a whip in each hand, throwing them high into the air and catching them again in the middle of a fast paced cracking routine. As a juggler this fascinated me. Years later, when I started cracking whips myself, I found that it is not as easy to accurately throw and catch a whip as it is a rigid object like a baton or a juggling club. However, I found one way that works fairly reliably. This is worth mastering, as it impresses an audience and adds visual variety to a whip cracking routine.

A short whip works best for this trick. While I have done it with my eight-foot (2.4m) whip, it is much easier with one under six feet (1.8m) in length. All the motion takes place in the shoulder wall plane.

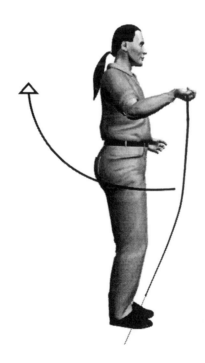

Chapter Eleven
Tricks and Stunts

Begin with a forward crack, and continue the follow through, so that the whip is rotating quickly in the shoulder wall plane. It should be travelling up behind you and down in front of you. You may wish to hold the knot of the whip in what club swingers call a ring grip, with the thumb and forefinger making a ring to hold the knot in place, but still allow it to rotate freely. This makes it easy to swing the whip without having to twist your wrist around.

When it has made one and a half revolutions from the forward crack, it should be horizontal in the air behind you and moving upwards. Let go of the handle.

The whip will go straight up in the air, turning over once. The handle will drop back into the palm of your upturned hand, in more or less the same position that you threw it from. Swing the whip forward half a revolution in the same direction as you were going before, and then do a reverse crack.

What Went Wrong?

- *The whip landed too far forward.* If you let go of the whip too late you will give it some forward momentum as well as the upward momentum.
- *The whip landed too far behind you.* You must have let go of it too early.
- *The whip did not turn enough.* You weren't rotating it fast enough.
- *The whip turned too much.* Work this one out for yourself.

Skip Your Whip

When the whip is rotating in the helicopter plane, bring it down to the floor while keeping it rotating. As it is about to hit your ankles, jump over it and take it back up to the helicopter plane again. Try mixing this move with overhead cracks and self wraps.

Chapter Twelve
Performance

What Next

If you've reached this point in the book, and you have learned, or at least tried, most of the moves I have described, you may be wondering what you should learn next. Well, you could pick up videos showing Aussie competitive two-handed stock whip work and start working on that. If you're more inclined to performance rather than competition, you could track down some videos of great performers like Vince Bruce, John Brady, or Joyce Rice, and start copying their tricks. But I don't think you should do either of these things. Let me explain why.

I regard whip cracking as an art, and art is not about copying other people. Oh, sure, it's fine to study the great masters, but only as a step on the way to developing your own style. I like it when other whip crackers impress me with something I haven't seen before. Now there are two ways you can do that. You can do it by doing whip cracking tricks that are so hard that it takes years of dedicated practice to learn them, or you can do it by making up something new. Now, it isn't easy to make up new things, but it's a lot easier than trying to copy Joyce Rice's act.

There's a story behind Joyce's act. She started her performing career as a baton twirler, and so many of her moves treat her whips as a baton with a firecracker at the end. She learned to crack whips from a person who stood perfectly still while cracking, so she had to apply her skills from baton twirling to choreograph her whip act. Volleys with a long whip she does two-handed because she did not have the strength to do it one-handed. If you copy her act you devalue both it and her story, and deny yourself the joy and sense of achievement that will come from going through your own creative process.

Making Stuff Up

Like many other things, creativity is a skill that can be learned and it is something you get better at if you practice. It amazes me when an otherwise intelligent person believes that it is difficult for them to come up with new ideas. Now, some people are naturally more creative than others, just as some have a better sense of balance or a better ear for music, but all of these skills can be developed by training and practice.

How do you learn to be creative? The trick is to come up with as many ideas as you can and then use the good ones. It's a two stage process. The first stage is brainstorming, writing down as many ideas as possible, without worrying about how stupid they are. Then you go through and pick out the ones that might work, and try them out.

There are several ways you can go about brainstorming — try them all and find out which ones work for you. This can be fun to do in a group. Set aside a time and say, "Okay, we are going to come up with three new whip moves today." This means you will have to come up with maybe fifty or sixty ideas, and throw away the vast majority.

It's important to write things down as you go, since that frees you to move on to the next idea. Here are some ways of coming up with new ideas. It's important not to rate ideas as good or bad at this stage. Just try to write down as many as possible. Even if your idea requires a live elephant, write it down.

Free Association

Just come up with random ideas about whips. This is the first thing most people think of when they think of brainstorming, and probably the hardest.

Free Association About a Random Word

Pick a word that has nothing to do with the subject in question — just open the dictionary at random and pick the first word you see. Then try to see how that word could apply to your problem. I just opened the dictionary on "grandfather." Now how would a grandfather crack a whip? What do grandfathers do? Take naps? Go fishing? Can I go fishing with a whip? Suppose I use one of those Japanese windsock fish, could I pick it up with a whip? Maybe if I attached a wire to the mouth I could wrap the whip round the wire and flick it into the air. "The fish are jumping today." "You should have seen the one that got away." Notice that we have come a long way from grandfather, but that doesn't matter. The idea was just to throw in a random element to help generate new ideas.

Opposites

Think of ways you can get to exactly the opposite of the effect you are looking for. This will set your mind going in unusual directions which will often generate ideas you would never have come up with if you had just been focused on your goal. Suppose your goal is to cut a target. Think of all the ways you could make it difficult to cut that target. Blindfolded, left handed, under the leg, behind the back, standing on your head, singing Ave Maria...

Transference

Take some move or trick from another discipline, and see if you can apply it to whips. I've taken moves from juggling, jazz dance, martial arts, club swinging, and poi, and applied them to whips. The move does not have to be an exact copy, but you can use it to inspire something new. Whatever else you like to do or to watch, be it skateboarding, yo-yo, ice skating, dance, gymnastics, bridge, or mah jong, try and pick one move from that discipline, and see if you can use it to inspire something in whip cracking.

Break Limits

Every skill has some unspoken assumptions. Pick one and see what happens if you break it. For instance, I might choose the assumption that I hold the handle of the whip in my hand. What happens if I let go of the handle? Can I throw and catch the whip? Sure, but in how many ways? What if the whip falls on the ground? Can I kick it up with my foot? Suppose I hold the handle with some other part of my body? Perhaps my elbow or mouth? Is it possible to crack a whip held between your toes? Can I hold the whip somewhere other than the handle? What moves can I do with a whip if I am holding the fall?

Impose Limits

Sometimes imposing an arbitrary limit can force creativity in new directions. For instance, when I was practicing at Circus Space in London a few years ago, I could not crack my whips very much as I was in a huge room with exposed brick walls (a former power station) and the noise would be most annoying to the other folks there. So, I was forced to come up with cool things to do with a whip that didn't involve actually cracking it. Some other limits you might try are changing planes after every crack (or keeping all cracks in the same plane), performing blindfolded, working with your back to the audience, turning 90 degrees after every crack, using a very long whip in one hand and a short one in the other...

Pick and Choose

When you have been brainstorming for a while, it's time to stop and pick the ideas you want to try. It's a good idea to organize the list into categories. It doesn't matter what the categories are, so long as they make sense to you. Then go through the stupid impossible ones, and see if you can make them possible. Maybe it doesn't have to be a live elephant; maybe it could be a stuffed one, or the family dog. Maybe you could rent the elephant.

Then go through and circle the ones you want to try. Then finally, get out there and try them. I'll look forward to seeing the results.

Getting Your Act Together

Many whip crackers will be happy just cracking whips, but I know that some of you will want to show off your skills to other people. Even if you have no interest in stage performance and will only be cracking whips for a few friends in your back yard, you should still try to present your skills in the best possible way. Here are some tips.

Keep It Short

There are very few people out there who have the attention span for a fifteen minute whip act. Almost everyone will enjoy a three minute act, even if you can't fit every single trick you know into that. Keep your act short and leave your audience wanting more.

Start With Your Second Best Trick

You want to start with something to grab the attention of your audience. This need not be anything really difficult, just something attention getting. A couple of really loud cracks may be enough. Don't keep up a high level of volume for the entire act, though. You don't want to deafen your audience or damage your whips.

Finish With Your Best Trick

Once again, your best trick is not the one that is most difficult; it's the one that looks the best to your audience. If you're not sure which one this is, just ask your audience after the show what they liked best. It's important that the last trick in your act is one that you can do every single time you try it. Few things leave a worse impression on an audience than a performer who ends with a failed trick.

Don't Take Risks

Don't try tricks that you can only do some of the time. The audience does not want to see you practice. Make sure everything in your act is solid. If you do miss a move, then it's okay to try it again, but never try anything more than three times. Just do a simpler version of the trick, or move on to the next thing. It is possible to build tension with the audience by failing on a trick twice and nailing it on the third attempt. If you want to do this, it's best to do a trick you can do every time, and miss deliberately on the first two attempts.

Do Something Funny

Even if you only pull a funny face when something goes wrong (or something goes right) then you should try to have some humor in your act. This is something that you can develop over time, but always be on the look out for ways to get laughs.

Let Your Act Evolve

Evolution really works and it will make your act better over time. All you need are random mutations and natural selection.

The random mutations are changes in your act. These may happen naturally because you don't remember how you meant to do your act, or someone in the audience shouts something out, or something goes wrong. You can also help the process by trying different things in your act, to see if the change improves it. You don't have to change your entire act; just try saying or doing one thing in a different way every time you perform.

The natural selection part means keeping the things that work, and not repeating the things that don't work. If something happens in your act that gets a good audience reaction, then make a note of it after you come offstage, and remember to do it every time from then on.

Costume, Character, Props, and Music

I've left the best trick until last. The person up on stage is not you. It is a character that you are playing. The character can be quite similar to you or completely different, but you should give conscious thought to who they are and how they behave. Everything else about your act should match that character. If your character is a cowboy then wear a cowboy's clothes and use Country Western music. If you choose a science fiction theme, then paint your whips silver and use music that suggests outer space. (Anything but the theme music from *Star Wars*, please. I have a kid who is a fan, and I have heard it far too many times.)

Practice wearing your costume. There's nothing worse than discovering that your fringed vest gets in the way of your Tasmanian cutbacks while you are in front of an audience. Also, make sure you check out your performance space before the show to make sure that it is big enough to do your whip act without bringing down the lights.

Finally, even if you are coaxed into an impromptu performance in the back yard with no costume or music or anything, remember to smile a lot and keep your tongue in your mouth. If it looks like you are having a good time your audience will as well.

Chapter Thirteen
Caring for Your Whip

If you look after a high-quality whip properly, it will last you a lifetime. Even low-quality whips will last longer if you look after them. Here are some things to avoid, and then some maintenance tips.

Don'ts

- *Don't bend or work your whip excessively.* If it is too stiff, the best way to break it in is to use it.
- *Don't coil your whip too tight.* You should not have to use any force to coil it for storage.
- *Don't crack your whip too loud.* This is impressive to people who don't know any better, but it will shorten the life of the whip, and you will run through poppers and falls in no time. A true whip master has the control to crack a whip quietly but perfectly every time.
- *Don't expose a leather whip to too much sunlight.* What's bad for your skin is also bad for leather.
- *Don't let a leather whip get wet.* If it does, hang it up by the handle to dry, and give it a treatment of leather dressing when it has dried out.
- *Don't let your whip get dirty.* Grit and dirt can work their way into the whip and wear away at the leather like sandpaper. If your whip does get dirty, wipe it down with a slightly damp cloth after use. Nylon whips can be washed with soap and water.
- *Don't treat a leather whip with Neats foot or mink oil.* This softens the leather, but it will eventually weaken the whip.
- *Don't crack your whip while standing on an abrasive surface like concrete or asphalt.* If you must, then stick to the overhead and other cracks where the whip is not dragged on the ground.
- *Don't leave your whip where pets or vermin can get at it.* To your puppy it looks (and smells) just like a chew toy. Rats, mice and roaches may also be attracted to the fat in the leather dressing, though some dressing will contain kerosene or other chemicals to discourage them.

The Whip Owner's Toolkit

There are a few common tools that you will need to look after your whips. This is what has ended up in my prop bag over the years. You may want to put together a similar set and take it with you when you practice, so you can conduct repairs on the spot. I'll explain how you use them all later.

- *A small container of conditioner.*
- *A couple of spare falls.*
- *A few poppers.*

- *Baling twine, nylon mason's twine and upholstery thread for making poppers.* Mostly I use baling twine.
- *Scissors.*
- *A fid for removing knots.*
- *A sharp knife.*
- *A small pair of pliers.* A leathermans tool or one similar will work fine for this.
- *A candle and a lighter.*
- *Balloons and polystyrene strips to use as targets.*
- *Parachute cord, for replacing falls on nylon whips.*
- *Electrical tape.* This is actually for repairing my juggling clubs and does not belong on this list at all, but it ended up in the same bag as all the whip tools.
- *A clothes peg.* With that and the electrical tape you can improvise a target holder pretty much anywhere and you can also use it as a candlestick if you want to try candle snuffing.

Conditioning Leather

Treat a leather whip every six months or so with a fatty leather dressing. The traditional Australian dressing consists mostly of rendered down mutton fat (also known as tallow) with additives like beeswax, grated Sunlight soap and kerosene. If you don't want to have your kitchen smelling of dead sheep for a couple of hours while you are brewing tallow, then you can buy Pecard leather dressing from some whip vendors, or use saddle soap. If you use a cake of hard saddle soap, grate it and make a paste with a little water. You may also find soft saddle soap next to the shoe polish in your local drug store. Cheap hand lotion may also work if you don't mind your whip smelling of perfume.

Using your fingers, rub the dressing into the whip. It doesn't take very much. The fall and the thin part of the thong may need more dressing than the handle end of the whip, as the belly acts as a reservoir for the fat. (So does my belly!). The oils from your hands naturally condition the handle as you use the whip, too. After you have treated the whole whip, hang it by the handle overnight, and in the morning, give it a rub with a soft dry cloth, to remove any excess, and polish it up. After a while you will be able to tell by the dry feel of your whip when it needs conditioning.

Washing and Waxing Nylon

Nylon whips will pick up dirt and grime more than leather whips. However, you can wash them with a mild detergent, and if you are really picky scrub them with a nail brush. Rinse and hang them up by the handle to dry.

Most makers of nylon whips soak them in paraffin wax. This makes them resistant to water and also gives them a little extra weight. The paraffin wax will eventually wear off. I don't bother to replace it as I usually practice indoors, but if you use your nylon whip in a wet climate you may wish to wax it from time to time.

First wash and dry the whip so that you are not sealing any dirt into it. Use ordinary household paraffin wax, and melt it in a double boiler. Don't heat it directly on the stove or it may get too hot and catch fire. When the wax has all melted, remove it from the heat, soak the whip in it for about ten minutes and hang it up by the handle to set. It will take a while for the wax in the middle of the whip to harden. Make sure the whip is hanging straight from the handle, or it may change the whip's performance.

Removing Knots

Check frequently for knots in your popper or fall. If you leave them in for a few cracks they get pulled so tight they can be difficult to remove. I carry a fid, which is a metal spike with a wooden handle. You can work the tip into a knot to loosen it up. They were originally a sailors' tool for working with ropes. They come in various shapes and sizes, but for whips I use a small one with a curved tip. Some folks would call this an awl, but I prefer to reserve that term for a tool with a sharp point, that you would use for punching holes in things.

Replacing the Popper

You will need to replace your popper quite often, as it wears down with use. After a particularly loud crack with a new popper you will sometimes see a little puff of fibers in the air at the point where the whip cracked.

Poppers can be attached in various ways. On some short snake whips the popper is braided into the end of the thong. Replacement of these is best left to a professional whip maker. Whips with Texas-style falls often have a hole in them through which the cracker is tied with a lark's head knot. If your whip has a nylon fall, it may be a single strand, in which case the end may start to fray. If it does, just hold the end in a candle flame for a few minutes to fuse it together. Another form of nylon fall is a loop twisted together, in which case you just tie the popper on with a lark's head knot, as you would for a fall with a hole in it.

In case you're not familiar with knots, to tie a lark's head you put the loop at the end of the cracker through the hole in the fall, then thread the tufted end of the popper through the loop and pull tight. There, done.

With an Australian style fall the popper is usually attached with a knot that is similar to a sheet bend.

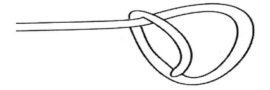

Work some conditioner into the end of the fall to soften it and make a loop in it. Fold the end of the fall so that it rests across the loop but does not go through it. The tip of the fall should just be resting on the edge of the loop.

Slip the loop on the popper up through the loop in the fall and over its tip.

Now pull the loop in the fall tight around the popper, then pull on the popper to make sure it is firmly tied on. Trim the tip of the fall with a very sharp knife so that it is flush with the edge of the loop.

If you are using an older popper which has lost its last few inches, you may find your knot getting bigger and bigger. In that case you can use a sharp knife to thin the end of the fall and get a smaller knot.

Making Poppers

You can buy poppers ready-made, but it is cheap and easy to make your own. I usually make about a dozen at a time, so I always have spares handy.

Traditionally silk was the favored material. A weather-beaten Australian stockman might ride into town and buy a single silk handkerchief to be shredded and twisted into poppers. Horsehair or other fibers might be used if silk was not available. These days we use nylon or polypropylene. One whip maker I know recommends Kevlar poppers if you want to cut targets, but I find them to be too brittle for everyday use.

Nylon will last longer than poly, but poly poppers are far less likely to foul or tangle or tie themselves in knots. A good source of polypropylene is the baling twine used on hay bales. Go anywhere they use hay bales and you will find lots of it for the taking. Baling twine is too thick to make a popper as is, but it is easy to split it and pull off a few strands to twist together.

This is the way I make a popper. Take about sixteen inches (0.4m) of thin nylon or poly string, and loop it over a hook on the wall, so that the ends are of equal length.

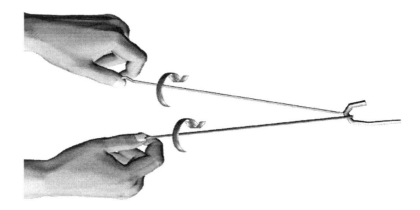

Now, each strand must be twisted, while keeping it separate from the other one. You can do this by rolling the strands between your fingers. If the string already consists of two or more strands twisted together, I usually twist it in the direction it is already twisted, but I have come across other people who untwist it instead, so I presume both ways work.

When you start to feel quite a bit of resistance to further twisting, hold the strands together and tie an overhand knot close to the ends. When you release the popper, the two strands should wrap around each other. You can trim the length of the tuft at the end to your preference. I like them to be a little less than an inch (2cm) but other people prefer them longer.

If you don't have a handy hook, you can pull the string straight between your hands to twist it up, then take the middle in your teeth, and fold it in half keeping it taut. Open your mouth and it should twist up a treat.

Replacing a Leather Fall

The tip of a leather fall undergoes a lot of stress, and every so often will break off, flinging a small leather knot away from you at the speed of sound. You can simply attach a new popper to the end of the fall, and continue using the whip. Some people like to use a longer popper as the fall gets shorter. After you have lost a few inches, however, it is time to replace the fall.

Buy a new fall from your favorite whip maker, and coat it with leather dressing. Before you take the old fall off, thread the old fall through the slit in the end of the new fall and pull it through until the new fall is on the thong of the whip. Slip a fid through the slit in the old fall where it goes around the thong, and pull the old fall backwards through the knot slightly, so that you can slip a sharp blade inside the loop and cut it. Now take the skinny end of the old thong and pull it out of the knot. If you do this right, the knot will still be there and you can push the thin end of the new fall through it. That's the tricky bit done.

Pull the new fall until about half of it is through the knot, then tighten up the knot a bit by pulling one at a time on the strands of leather coming out of it. You can use a small pair of pliers for this. You may notice that one strand is longer than the others. This one gets doubled back and threaded through the slit in the fall when you pull it the rest of the way through, to lock the knot in place.

The very end of the thong, right before the fall is attached, is another major stress point, and can often start to wear. Ask your whip maker to unbraid the end of your whip and shorten it by about 1/8 inch (3mm) if you see this happening. That way the worn parts of the strands will be moved to a point where they are not under stress.

Replacing a Nylon Fall

Generally a nylon fall will last a lot longer than a leather fall, unless the popper comes off and you don't notice, or you regularly crack the whip too loud or use it on an abrasive surface. If you do subject your whips to this sort of abuse you should repent and mend your ways, but if that fails, here's how you fix the problem.

Some nylon whips are made just like leather whips, and the fall consists of a strand of parachute cord doubled in half and twisted. You can replace this in just the same way as you do a leather fall. Parachute cord is normally only sold in huge quantities, so it is probably cheaper to order new falls from your whip maker than to buy the cord and make your own.

Other nylon whips have a single strand of parachute cord as a fall. This is tied onto the end of the thong. The very tip of the thong is slightly thicker so the fall does not slip off. To replace this, cut off the old fall. Be careful not to damage the thong as you do this. Now take a length of parachute cord about a foot (0.3m) longer than you want the new fall to be, fuse both ends with a candle flame, and tie it on. Trim both ends so the fall is the right length and the knot is neat, and fuse them with the candle flame again.

The knot you should use goes like this. Lay about two inches (5cm) of the fall parallel to the end of the thong, with the rest of the fall extending beyond the end of the whip. Take the end that extends beyond the end of the whip and wrap it four times round both the fall and the thong, working your way back down towards the handle. Now thread the long end of the fall back up through the four loops you have made and pull tight. The loops should lie neatly next to each other.

Chapter Fourteen
Whips as Weapons

Blacksnakes

Most of the whips that are cracked today evolved just for making a noise, to herd cattle or perhaps to control sled dogs. Usually they are not intended to hit anything or anyone. If you use a whip to hit livestock, you run the risk of doing too much damage, breaking bones or leaving open wounds that may get infected. There is one type of whip that has a more sordid history, though, and that is the short blacksnake. Part whip and part blackjack, it is a vicious street fighting weapon.

A blackjack (also called a cosh outside the U.S.) is a small club with a flexible handle and a lead weight on the end, usually with a leather cover. A light tap on the skull with one of these is enough to render the victim unconscious, and a full force hit will break bones. In many jurisdictions it is illegal to carry one.

Some time ago, probably in the early 19th century, a canny whip maker had the bright idea of loading the handle of a short snake whip with lead shot and selling it for use as a blackjack. While there might be a law against carrying a blackjack, there was no law against walking around with a whip rolled up in your pocket. Often these whips will have some fancy plaiting beginning three or four inches (75mm to 100mm) into the thong. This is to give a better grip when the whip is reversed and used as a club. If the whip is grasped a bit further down the thong, then the handle can be swung like a nunchuck, too.

Blacksnakes have attracted the attention of luminaries from Mark Twain to Russ Meyer. In *The Galaxy*, December 1870, Mark Twain wrote, "How well I remember my grandmother's asking me not to use tobacco, good old soul! She said, 'You're at it again, are you, you whelp? Now, don't ever let me catch you chewing tobacco before breakfast again, or I lay I'll black snake you within an inch of your life!' I have never touched it at that hour of the morning from that time to the present day."

A century later, Russ Meyer's movie *Black Snake: The Whip* told the story of a slave revolt on a Caribbean island. Instead of Meyer's usual exploitation of female anatomy, this film used the crack of the whip for its shock appeal.

The Danger Zone

A whip is at its most dangerous at the moment it cracks, and it is usually fully extended when this happens. For a short whip the danger zone is between four and six feet (1.2m to 1.8m) from the whip handler. If you are facing an opponent with a short whip in a fight, you have two options. You can run away, or you can move closer and attempt to punch, kick, or grapple with the whip handler. If you are closer than four feet (1.2m), you are too close to be easily hit by the cracking end of a whip, but watch out for a quick flip or a switch to the other hand to turn that whip into a blackjack.

Short whip fighters will usually retreat from someone who tries to grapple with them, while dealing quick stinging blows aimed at both sides of the head and torso. When a blow connects and the pain distracts the opponent, the whip handler can then reverse the whip and use the handle for a disabling blow.

The best cracks to use for short whip fighting are variations of the sidearm and overhand flick. A whip handler should avoid moves like the forward crack, which have a long setup and thus telegraph his intentions to an opponent. Strokes may alternate from the left and right hand sides or stay on the same side of the body. In either case, the follow through from one stroke must be the setup for the next. The whip should be continually moving in ever changing unpredictable vertical and diagonal planes. Moves in a pure horizontal plane should be avoided unless the whip is very stiff, as the follow through may wrap around and hit the whip handler on the back. Even if the whip is not travelling fast enough to be painful at this point it takes too long to reverse the motion and bring the whip back to fighting mode, and it is quite undignified.

The basic exercises you should practice if you want to defend yourself with a short whip are the continuous overhand flick on both sides of your body, and the X pattern where you flick the whip from upper whip side to low on the other side, then from high on the other side to low on the whip side. By switching from one pattern to another and varying angles and timing you can create an intimidating defensive screen of fast moving leather.

Other Short Whips

One way that a whip fighter can prevent someone moving inside the danger zone is to use a knife in the other hand. Whip and knife techniques are taught in Filipino martial arts such as Kali. One form of whip traditionally used was the buntot pagi or tail of a stingray! The poison was left in the sting making this a particularly vicious weapon.

A weapon called the sjambok originated in Southern Africa, and is now widely available. It's similar to a whip in that it is a flexible tapered hand weapon between about three to five feet (0.9m to 1.5m) in length. However, the sjambok is not flexible enough to crack and does not have a popper. It is only intended as a weapon, and is carried by South African police for riot control, instead of the nightstick or truncheon we are familiar with in the U.S. Originally they were made from a single strip of thick hippopotamus hide, rounded by rolling between steel plates and tapered from a little over one inch (25mm) in diameter down to three eighths of an inch (9mm). These days cheap but effective plastic versions are common and can be found for a few dollars on eBay. The hippo versions sometimes turn up there too, selling for fifty dollars or more. Being more rigid than a genuine whip they are easier to control, and thus require less training to use effectively.

I have seen a whip with two metal rings at the handle end, which allow it to be fastened round your waist and used as a belt. Note that unless you have spent a number of hours practicing the use of a whip, pepper spray is likely to provide a more effective form of defense, if it is legal in your jurisdiction. The other advantage of pepper spray is that when you take it out to use it, your pants don't fall down.

Longer Whips

Longer whips can be used as weapons, but they require a different set of techniques. As well as striking, the whip can be used to wrap a body or limb and disarm an opponent or pull them off balance. A wrap aimed at about knee height followed by a sharp tug on the whip will bring most people to their knees.

It takes an appreciable amount of time to set up and crack a long whip, and the danger zone is further away from the whip handler. An opponent who judges the timing correctly can avoid the blow and then step inside the whip handler's danger zone before he has time to set up another crack. At this point the whip handler has several options.

As with a short whip, a knife can be held in the other hand to discourage a close approach, or the handle of the whip can be used as a club. However, the extra length of the thong allows additional moves. The handle can be thrown or swung while holding on to the thong. Many techniques used in Kung Fu for a weapon called the rope dart can be used with a reversed whip. If you've never seen a rope dart, look out for the movie *Shanghai Noon* where Jackie Chan improvises one out of a lariat and a horseshoe.

The length and rigidity of a bullwhip or cow whip handle allow it to be used as you would a stick, to block blows with other weapons, or to hit and thrust. There's another possibility, too. If the whip handler can flip a loop of the thong over the opponent's head, pulling on the thong and pushing with the handle held horizontally will result in a chokehold, or if done forcefully can crush a windpipe. (Chokeholds can be extremely dangerous. Do not attempt to practice them without coaching from an experienced martial arts master.)

A loop of the whip can be used in other ways. If the thong is doubled back and held in the same hand as the handle it can deliver a powerful blow, extending the reach of an arm. If an opponent tries to kick, it can be hooked around an incoming leg and used to pull him off balance.

But Seriously...

Overall, though, in spite of the emotional and artistic appeal (and if you don't think whips are appealing why are you reading this book?), long whips are not the most effective weapons for self-defense. I asked a black belt friend of mine who also cracks whips if she would rather face an opponent with or without a whip in her hand. She responded, "Having something in hand is always nice — I'd rather hit hard things like skulls with something other than a fragile hand. And it would be helpful in making a safe getaway — being able to back off and keep him at a distance would be helpful (or at least it would if my aim were better). I can think of ways I could use a bullwhip, for example, to remove a knife from a hand. But would I, as a choice? Probably only in limited situations — like someone with a knife standing just outside my kicking range, where I could hit the hand with the butt end (hiding the swing with my body — the perfect set-up is needed) or with the end, and do a wrap. I think using the bullwhip is like jujitsu rather than karate — in karate, you have a few dozen techniques, most of which can be used in pretty much any situation. In jujitsu you have hundreds of techniques, each applicable to only particular set-ups and attacks."

The sound of a whip crack will grab the attention of a room full of people, and the whip can then be used as a threat to control a group, especially if a long whip is cracked over their heads. However, the sound can also be mistaken for that of a gun. A friend of mine was cracking his whip in Golden Gate Park in San Francisco one day, when a police officer came over and asked him to stop because he kept mistaking it for gunfire and it was making him jumpy. It's not healthy to be around nervous cops, so my friend postponed his practice session for another day.

Whipmaker Gayle Nemeth, from Queensland, Australia, is promoting the sport of full contact whip fighting. Contestants wear long heavy coats and fencing masks, and whack away at each other with stock whips. Points are scored for a clean strike to the head only, so the object of the game is to avoid or block your opponent's blows, while setting up a clean hit yourself. Gayle's sparring partner, Angie Mooney says, "Even though you are protected the sound of the whips hitting is frightening and you can't help flinching as the whip cracks around you! It's amazing!"

Perhaps the most amusing method for self-defense using a whip goes as follows. First do your most impressive and stylish multiple crack routine to keep your attacker at bay. Then pretend to accidentally drop your whip. Now stand back and watch while your attacker picks up your whip and injures himself with it!

Chapter Fifteen
A Note on History

The First Whips

The origins of whip cracking are lost in history. After all, we're all familiar with the image of whip wielding overseer bullying the gang of slaves into dragging those huge stone blocks to build the pyramids, right? In fact, when I checked this with an Egyptologist, I was told that this could not be further from the truth. The work crews building the pyramids were generally not slaves, but farmers and farm workers. The pyramids were vast government public works programs intended to give the agricultural classes something to do while their farmland was flooded by the Nile. Also, there is no evidence that the Egyptians had a whip that cracked. For punishment they used sticks, for horses a riding-crop, and for driving cattle a short flail.

In fact the first supersonic cracks on earth may predate the Egyptians by a hundred and fifty million years. Recent research by cyberpaleontologist Nathan Myhrvold, formerly head of basic research at Microsoft, suggests that the long tapering tail of the Apatasaurus could crack like a whip. A computer model of the 30-ton dinosaur indicates that with only one fifth of the energy required to walk, it could make the end of its tail break the sound barrier. Imagine a 40 foot (12m) long tail weighing 3,200 pounds (1,450kg) cracking at 200 decibels!

While some have suggested that this tail may have been used as a weapon, Myhrvold believes that it was used for sexual display. "Most of the outlandish things that animals have are due to sexual selection," he says. I don't know if hanging around cracking a whip would have helped you to find a sexual partner in the Late Jurassic Period, but there are some people trying it in contemporary San Francisco. Maybe one day we'll find a dinosaur skeleton with fossil chaps!

Old Testament

There is a reference to whip cracking in the *Old Testament*, in the *Book of Nahum 2:3*. It's from a description of the sounds made by an avenging army approaching the sinful city of Nineveh. "The crack of whip, and rumble of wheel, galloping horse and bounding chariot!" (Revised Standard Version.) Okay, I admit I'd never heard of the *Book of Nahum* until I looked it up, but there it is tucked between *Micah* and *Habakkuk*.

The *King James edition* of the *Bible* translates this as, "The noise of a whip..." though. The earliest use of the word "crack" that I can find applied to whips is from Stapylton's 1647 translation of Juvenal, "The carter cracks his whip." A more literal translation of the line from Juvenal would be, "The mule driver has been signaling with his switch," so the Latin text does not necessarily imply that the whip was being cracked.

The Classical World

As far as I can determine, the ancient Greeks charioteers used a straight whip about four feet (1.2m) long. It was probably similar to a quirt or riding crop, and I doubt if it cracked. There's a long description of a chariot race in Homer's *Illiad*, but no mention of whip cracking.

By Roman times charioteers used a whip with a rigid handle a foot or two (30cm to 60cm) in length, attached to a thong perhaps two or three feet (60cm to 90cm) long. This may not have cracked, though it made a handy weapon against the other chariots in the more fiercely contested races. Carters used a longer whip of similar construction, similar to a modern lunge whip. It's quite possible that this would crack.

I have found one reference to whip cracking in Roman literature. In Virgil's *Aeneid*, Book V, Line 579 it says, "Epytides longe dedit insonuitque flagello." The important bit is the last two words, "Insonuitque flagello" which translates as, "And he sounded a riding whip." "Insono" is a verb meaning to make a loud or reverberating sound. It's used mostly in poems of rhetoric, and not something you would come across in everyday speech. The "uit" ending gives the tense and person. The "que" bit is the same as putting "and" before the phrase. "Flagellum" is a diminutive form of "Flagrum," a whip or lash, so we have the idea that this is a smaller whip, probably a riding whip of some sort. The "o" ending just says that the whip is being used to crack, rather than being the subject of the sentence. Epytides is the name of a person. He was signaling the start of a cavalry display by shouting and cracking his whip, so this was a ceremonial display of some sort. The *Aeneid* was written about 19 BCE, during the reign of the Emperor Augustus.

European Traditions

Whip cracking plays a part in a number of European folk traditions, often relating to either spring or midwinter festivals.

In Slavic countries the first release of the cattle into the summer pasture on St. George's Day (May 6th) could be the occasion for a number of rituals, including whip cracking to frighten away witches or demons. In Romania on New Year's Eve, children may go from house to house ringing bells, cracking a long whip and offering the seasons greetings. Again, the purpose is probably to frighten off evil spirits. In parts of southern Germany children with whips and bells may be making the rounds in a similar fashion on the three Thursdays before Christmas.

Near the border between Germany and Austria, in the Rupertiwinkel or Salzburg districts, there is an annual competition called the Aperschnalzen, which means "open whip cracking." Teams of competitors crack whips in front of a panel of seven judges, who award marks based on the sound of the crack. From the description I have seen it appears that only the overhead crack is used. After the competition, all five or six hundred entrants crack their whips at the same time! The festival is held in spring every year and the contestants are all unmarried men. Maybe they are all in search of a meaningful relationship with an Apatasaurus.

The village of Hallwil in Switzerland holds a whip-cracking contest called the Chlauswettchloöpfe around the start of December every year, as part of an extended winter festival. Around thirty participants in three age groups compete with whips up to sixteen feet (5m) long to win a pewter pitcher. A couple of weeks later the whip crackers of Hallwil are out again for the Chlausjage or pursuit of St. Nicholas. Six costumed teenage boys with whips visit the children of the village to give gifts to the good ones and warn the naughty ones!

The Klausjagen (same meaning, different spelling) is also celebrated in another Swiss village, Kussnacht. On December 5th every year, whip crackers lead a parade of two hundred townspeople carrying huge lanterns in the shape of bishop's miters, who escort St. Nicholas into town for the holiday season. This is apparently a tamer version of an older celebration, when St. Nicholas was chased through the town by the local youths wielding whips.

In northern England, rushes were used as floor coverings until the mid-nineteenth century. The annual rush harvest in summer was celebrated by a festival called Wakes or Rushbearing. A decorated cart full of rushes would be dragged through the streets by a team of young men, escorted by whip crackers, morris dancers, musicians, and young women wearing garlands. According to Fishwick's History of Rochdale, the whips used "were made of rope and string, the lash being five feet long and the handle about eighteen inches, and when skillfully used the result was a crack as loud as a pistol shot." Another longer and heavier form of whip was also used, which required two hands to crack.

Asian Traditions

In Sri Lanka every August, precious relics of the Buddha are paraded through the streets in a procession called the Kandy Esala Perahera. Whip crackers add to the festivities, along with stilt walkers, dancers, drummers and magnificently decorated elephants. I don't know of any other examples of whip cracking in Asian festivals, but I'd be happy to hear of them.

A friend brought me a modern whip from Tibet. It's an eight-plait bullwhip in white leather with a wooden handle painted gold, and a tuft of red fibers where the handle joins the thong. The braiding is fairly coarse and the belly is not heavy enough. The thong goes from being braided into three twisted sections of successively smaller diameter, which is a form of construction I had not come across before, though some cow whips do end in a single twisted section. It did not have a fall or popper, but when I added them it cracked quite happily.

Mechanized Whip Making

With the coming of the industrial revolution there was an increase in population, wealth and commerce. Until the development of the internal combustion engine, the horse was the main form of transportation within town, and also between any towns that the railway didn't reach. From the hansom cabs of Victorian London to the stagecoaches of the Wild West, all the coachmen would need some form of whip. The demand was enormous, but the town of Westfield, Massachusetts was able to meet the challenge.

To this day, Westfield is known to the locals as Whip City. In 1822, a Westfield man called Hiriam Hull invented a whip-making machine that could plait cotton thread around a tapered belly. The whip making industry exploded there, until the town was supplying 95% of the U.S. market, as well as much of the rest of the world. By 1893, forty two different whip making companies employed 80% of the labor force there, turning out tens of thousands of whips a day. With the coming of the automobile the industry declined rapidly, and only one company survives today. The Westfield Whip Manufacturing Company is still in business, though, mass producing equestrian whips with equipment some of which dates back to the 1860s.

The American Bullwhip

Whip manipulation was a source of pride for nineteenth century America. In 1844, Josiah A. Gregg described a wagon train from the United States about to arrive in Santa Fe: "There was yet another preparation to be made in order to 'show off' to advantage. Each wagoner must tie a brand new "cracker" to the lash of his whip; for, on driving through the streets and the plaza publica, every one strives to outvie his comrades in the dexterity with which he flourishes this favorite badge of his authority."

The bullwhip and stock whip as we know them today were both developed for herding cattle on the open range, rather than driving horses. Europe had no need of cowboys, with its dense population, fenced pastures and intensive farming. Whips were only used in the mountainous regions there. However, when faced with ranching the wide open spaces of America and Australia, European settlers were forced to develop or rediscover different techniques and create new tools, so that for most of the year one man and a horse could handle a thousand head of cattle.

The early settlers in the American West and the Native Americans before them used rawhide for all manner of construction projects and repairs. I like to think of it as cowboy duct tape! It was used for braiding everyday ropes and whips as well as bridles and other equestrian gear, some of it of tremendous beauty and elegance. Today you can still find rawhide bullwhips if you shop carefully, but it is hard to work with rawhide, so not many whip makers have mastered that art.

The bullwhip bears some resemblance to the lariats used for roping cattle. It was swung around overhead, and would coil up in the saddlebag just like a lariat. It was even braided in the same way from the same material, for lariat comes from the Spanish "la reata," a rawhide rope. In fact, much of the style and techniques of Western braiding came from people of Spanish ancestry, and the Spaniards had in turn learned from the Moors during the Moorish occupation of Spain.

The Australian Stock Whip

In Australia, meanwhile, the settlers also used rawhide but were soon to discover that in kangaroo hide they had the ultimate leather for whip making, in strength, density and durability. Australian whip makers found that with roo hide they could cut thinner strands of leather lace and braid in more intricate patterns than had been possible before. If Whip City in the U.S. brought mechanized whip making to its high point, Australian craftsmen did the same for hand braiding.

The Australian stock whip seems to have evolved from English carriage whips, though the handle got a little shorter, and the thong longer and better weighted. The terms "stock whip" and "bullwhip" first appeared in print in the mid-nineteenth century, though they were probably in use by cattlemen well before that. Australia produced bullwhips too, but they were mainly made for export to America, and often had a longer cane, so they handled more like stock whips.

The Twentieth Century

Whip makers still talk about the Great Depression as the time when whip making reached its highest development. Perhaps it was because the whip makers had so few orders that they could afford to lavish the greatest care and attention on each one, or perhaps all but the best craftsmen were driven out of the business for lack of work. Whatever the reason, the whip makers of that time set a high standard for future generations.

Today there seems to be a great upsurge in interest in whips and whip making. High quality whips are more available than they have been in fifty years, and the demand for them keeps increasing. It seems as if the future of the ancient art of whip cracking is assured.

Chapter Sixteen
Other Resources

Associations and Meetings

The Wild West Arts Club is an American organization for devotees of whip cracking, lariat, knife throwing, gun spinning, trick riding, and other cowboy skills. They publish a newsletter and hold regional conventions, as well as an annual convention, which features workshops, shows, and competitions. Many of the best whip crackers in the world turn up. For more information see http://www.wwac.com/ or mail Wild West Arts Club, 3750 S Valley View #14, Las Vegas, NV 89103.

The Australian Plaiters and Whipmakers Association is open to whip makers and whip enthusiasts in all countries. Its newsletter, *The Australian Whipmaker*, is full of whip lore and history, as well as practical whip making and braiding advice. If you are ordering a whip internationally from Australia, I would recommend that you only buy from current members of the Association, as they are willing to mediate any business disputes. For more information see http://www2.tpg.com.au/users/ramskull/ or mail 12 Fairyland Rd, Kuranda, Qld 4872, Australia.

The Whip Enthusiasts Group is an Internet mailing list currently hosted at http://groups.yahoo.com/group/WhipEnthusiasts/. Some of the best whip crackers and whip makers in the world are to be found there, as well as amateurs at all levels of skill. There are also local meetings in a number of cities. See http://www.WhipEnthusiasts.org/ for details.

Books

I don't know of any other books on the subject of whip cracking, which is why I wrote this one! If you are interested in making your own whips, however, here are some suggestions.

How to Make Whips, by Ron Edwards, 1997, Cornell Maritime Press, $24.95. The author is the founder of the Australian Plaiters and Whipmakers Association, and has been working for years to record and preserve traditional crafts. This work may be the inspiration for a new generation of whip makers. Though the emphasis is on Australian stockwhips, other styles are covered. Techniques described go from basic whips up to fancy work like braiding a name into a handle. There are many detailed illustrations that help to make this the best book for beginners to learn from. Ron thinks that you can't teach whip cracking from a book, but I hope I've proved him wrong!

Whips and Whipmaking, by David Morgan, 1972, Cornell Maritime Press, $9.95. David Morgan has done more than anyone else to keep fine whip making in America alive. In this book he shares his knowledge about many different varieties of whips and their uses, and tells about braiding and whip making. As well as Morgan's own advice, this book also contains a reprint of an English book on whip making first published in 1893.

Braiding Fine Leather, Techniques of the Australian Whipmakers, by David Morgan, 2002. Cornell Maritime Press, $19.95. This is a more detailed description of whip making technique by Morgan, which also has descriptions of simpler braiding projects which will help you develop your plaiting skills before attempting your first whip. This is similar to the traditional approach of apprenticeship with which Morgan is very familiar. Many of the current generation of American whip makers have apprenticed with Morgan.

Encyclopedia of Rawhide and Leather Braiding, by Bruce Grant, 1978, Cornell Maritime Press, $28.95. This book is the definitive work on leather braiding. It contains a few pages of instructions on making a bullwhip, though that is not its primary focus.

Videos

Western Stage Props sells a number of whip videos, some educational and some showing great whip crackers in practice and performance. See http://www.westernstageprops.com/ or mail Western Stage Props, 3750 S. Valley View, #14, Las Vegas, NV 89103 USA for a catalog.

Mike Murphy has made several excellent videos, now available on DVD, teaching the Australian competitive two-handed whip cracking style, as well as one on whip maintenance and repair. You can order them from him at http://www.murphywhips.com/ or they are available from Western Stage Props.

Anthony De Longis is an actor and stuntman who has appeared in numerous movies and TV shows. He also sells several videos of whip instruction. See http://www.delongis.com/ or mail Anthony De Longis, P.O. Box 3333, Hollywood, CA 90078-3333.

A number of movies have featured whip sequences, including *The Mask of Zorro*, the *Indiana Jones* movies, *Batman Returns*, *Catwoman*, *Underworld*, and *Rundown*. Typically whips of several different lengths will be used in a movie depending on the stunt, and the sound of the whip cracking will be added later, sometimes at completely the wrong time!

The Internet

I hope I may be excused a little nepotism if I refer you to the site that I edit, http://www.bullwhip.org/, the home of the Bullwhip FAQ. As well as containing information on a number of aspects of whips and whip cracking not covered in this book, I also try to maintain a link to every other related site I can find. This includes home pages of whip makers, professional performers, hobbyists and collectors. You can also find out about mailing lists and meetings there. Things change rapidly on the web, and many of the URLs I included in the first edition were out of date by the time I came to revise the book, but I'll try to keep Bullwhip.org reasonably up to date. If something listed here doesn't work…

The Whip Enthusiasts mailing list is a great place for gossip and questions, discussion of the merits of different whip makers, and notices of meetings and events.

Wow, you made it to the end. Thanks for reading my book.

YOU WILL ALSO WANT TO READ:

☐ **19216 The Scourge of the Dark Continent, The Martial Use of the African Sjambok, *by James Loriega, with a Foreword by James Keating.*** The sjambok is one of the most versatile and effective of all flexible weapons, having been used for centuries in Africa. The author has written the first book-length treatment of the defensive use of the sjambok. Loriega, a well-known and respected martial arts expert covers every aspect of the sjambok: it's history, how to practice; where to obtain a sjambok; and how to modify it so it is best for your personal use; and much, much more. *1999, 5½ x 8½, 143 pp, soft cover.* **$16.95.**

☐ **22044 Combat Knife Throwing, A New Approach to Knife Throwing and Knife Fighting, *by Ralph Thorn.*** Conventional wisdom among knife-fighting experts has it that knife throwing is a pursuit best left to circus performers, hillbilly theme parks, and hobbyists and that it is useless for combat and other survival purposes. In this ground-breaking new book, Ralph Thorn differentiates between "circus" knife throwing and *combat* knife throwing, and reveals his style of knife throwing suitable for actual combat and knife fights. The author shows you how to balance a knife for throwing; how to build your own targets; how to practice the various combat throwing techniques, and much more. *2003, 8½ x 5½, 114 pp, illustrated, soft cover.* **$15.00.**

☐ **19237 Cao Dai Kung-Fu: Lost Fighting Arts of Vietnam, *by Dr. Haha Lung.*** Dr. Haha Lung begins with an overview of the land and characteristics of the people, giving readers the basis for an understanding of Vietnam's history and how this contributed to the rise of the Cao Dai religion. The author reminds us that the word "martial" means "war." While there may be beauty in a perfectly performed practice session, this "art" aspect takes a backseat to the "martial" in a life and death struggle. The purpose of martial arts, after all, is to complement your war arsenal. In a battlefield situation, unarmed martial arts are what you use between weapons. The purpose of *Cao Dai Kung-Fu* is to teach you how to get that arsenal fully armed. To this end the martial arts instructions in this book are written in an easy to understand manner with helpful illustrations and diagrams, so that even one uninitiated in the martial arts can find useful tips to store away in preparation for self defense in general. *2002, 8½ x 11, 200 pp, illustrated, soft cover.* **$17.95.**

☐ **19203 The Sling: For Sport and Survival, *by Cliff Savage.*** A complete illustrated guide to making and using a sling — the ancient weapon David used to kill Goliath. Slings are silent, accurate and deadly. They are more powerful than a bow, and ammunition is free. Easily improvised and highly portable, they are increasingly used in urban guerrilla warfare, particularly in Northern Ireland and Israel's West Bank. Step-by-step, illustrated slinging stances, construction techniques and ammunition ideas highlight this book. *The Sling* is highly recommended for all survivalists and weapons enthusiasts. *1984, 5½ x 8½, 72 pp, illustrated, soft cover.* **$10.00.**

☐ **19201 Boxing's Dirty Tricks and Outlaw Killer Punches, *by J.C. "Champ" Thomas.*** Before there was "Ultimate Fighting," men like J.C. "Champ" Thomas made their livings beating each other senseless and occasionally dying in the ring. Beginning in 1923, Thomas' career as a boxer, wrestler, and boombattler has spanned nearly six decades! A veteran of over 10,000 bouts, Thomas successfully defended himself against some of the world's fiercest aggressors, and killed his opponents on several occasions. Now he shares his secrets with those who wish to study the real manly arts! Learn how to deter and overcome opponents by: using your gloves' laces as weapons; thumbing and elbowing your way to victory; breaking your victims' feet; dealing potent low blows; destroying your adversaries with resin; choking your foes; and much, much more. *1997, 5½ x 8½, 174 pp, illustrated, soft cover.* $15.00.

❏ **19219 How to Be an Ass-Whipping Boxer,** *by J.C. "Champ Thomas.* J.C. "Champ" Thomas has been an icon on the American boxing scene for decades. His books have been a step-by-step road map to success for countless boxers, whether they were beginners, amateurs, professionals or just someone who wanted to know more about boxing and the art of self-defense. Champ himself saw his boxing manuals as a way for aspiring boxers and pros alike to become first-rate contenders without spending hundreds or thousands of dollars on personal trainers or managers that may not deliver all that they promise. This volume is actually a compilation of some of Champ's best work, and provides both an overview of what it takes to win and in-depth instruction on how to do it. What were originally published as individual manuals are presented as sections of this book, sections that deal with various aspects of boxing and the art of self-defense. The books are presented essentially as written, complete with introductions written by admirers and former students. *2000, 8½ x 11, 165 pp, illustrated, soft cover.* $18.95.

❏ **19205 Kill-As-Catch-Can, Wrestling Skills for Streetfighting,** *by Ned Beaumont.* Sure, you know how to punch and kick, but how well can you fight at shorter range? Can you defend yourself when the right turns to grappling? When both you and your opponent are rolling around and wrestling on the barroom floor, are you confident that you can win the fight? If you doubt your chances at close quarters, then you're not prepared for the reality of streetfighting. That's because, as author Ned Beaumont points out, in the real world, fights frequently begin with or turn into bouts of wrestling, and the antagonist with the greater expertise in wrestling is most often the victor. *Kill-As-Catch-Can* is a no-nonsense primer that can effectively guide the reader to an enhanced awareness of wrestling methodology, and provide streetfighters with the edge it takes to come out on top. The truly tough customer is the person who thoroughly conditions himself, diligently studies and practices wrestling holds and techniques, and then makes full use of them in rough-and-tumble situations. Learn to prevail in the street! *1998, 5½ x 8½, illustrated, soft cover.* $16.95.

❏ **58144 Prison Killing Techniques,** *by Ralph Dean Omar. Anyone* whose lifestyle or job might conceivably bring them into contact with this nation's fastest growing prisons — and the subcultural survivalists who hunt there — will benefit from reading this graphic and shocking book. You may have *trained* for years to survive on foreign terrain, or *trained* for 20 years in karate or some other martial art. You may have very well trained, but inside the Steel Nation, *experience* is what counts. Do you know where to find and how to use the environmental weapons provided in your surroundings? Improvised weapons (and how to use them) are included in this book. *2001, 5½ x 8½, 132 pp, illustrated, soft cover.* $14.95.

❏ **88888 2005 Loompanics Unlimited Main Catalog.** The catalog is *FREE* with the purchase of any book, **$5.00** if ordered separately. See the catalog ad on the last page.

Please send me the books I have checked below:

❑ 19216, The Scourge of the Dark Continent, $16.95

❑ 22044, Combat Knife Throwing, $15.00

❑ 19237, Cao Dai Kung-Fu, $17.95

❑ 19203, The Sling, $10.00

❑ 19201, Boxing's Dirty Tricks and Outlaw Killer Punches, $15.00

❑ 19219, How to Be an Ass-Whipping Boxer, $18.95

❑ 19205, Kill-As-Catch-Can, $16.95

❑ 58144, Prison Killing Techniques, $14.95

❑ 88888, 2005 Loompanics Main Catalog, $5.00 (FREE with any book order).

NBWB5

LOOMPANICS UNLIMITED
PO BOX 1197
PORT TOWNSEND, WA 98368

Please send me the books I have checked above. I am enclosing $ _____ which includes $6.25 for shipping and handling of orders up to $25.00. Add $1.00 for each additional $25.00 ordered. *Washington residents please include 8.3% for sales tax.*

NAME _____

ADDRESS _____

CITY _____

STATE/ZIP _____

We accept Visa, Discover, MasterCard, and American Express.
To place a credit card order *only*,
call 1-800-380-2230, 24 hours a day, 7 days a week.
Or fax us your credit card order at: 1-360-385-7785
Or you can order online through our Web Site:
www.loompanics.com